GOD STILL SPEAKS

Bryce —
your journey is
valuable & precious
to God. Every story
matters.
Peggy

God Still Speaks

My Surprising Spiritual Journey In Knowing God

Peggy E. McCoy

XULON PRESS

Xulon Press
2301 Lucien Way #415
Maitland, FL 32751
407.339.4217
www.xulonpress.com

© 2019 by Peggy E. McCoy

All rights reserved solely by the author. The author guarantees all contents are original and do not infringe upon the legal rights of any other person or work. No part of this book may be reproduced in any form without the permission of the author. The views expressed in this book are not necessarily those of the publisher.

Unless otherwise indicated, Scripture quotations taken from the Holy Bible, New International Version (NIV). Copyright © 1973, 1978, 1984, 2011 by Biblica, Inc.™. Used by permission. All rights reserved.

Edited by Xulon Press.

Printed in the United States of America.

ISBN-13: 978-1-54566-100-0

*Therefore My people shall know My name;
Therefore they shall know in that day
That I am He who speaks:
"Behold, it is I."*

(Isaiah 52:6 NKJV)

Endorsements

I have the great honor to introduce you to a book that I am confident will help you draw closer to God. This is so much more than a book. In a beautifully profound way, Peggy draws you into the reality that God Still Speaks, and He wants to speak to us all. I have known Peggy for a decade now, and I know her to be a woman of sincerity. Her faith and relationship with God is infectious, and leaps off the pages of this book. I encourage you to lean in with an open heart. I pray that you find the same experience in your journey with God as my dear friend Peggy.

Pastor John Caravalho
Mission City Church, Santa Clara
www.mc.church/

Peggy McCoy wrote from her heart. This book will assure you that God always speaks to His children. Her story will inspire you to pursue a deeper relationship with Jesus.

    I had the privilege of being her pastor many years ago. I remember her asking me about writing some deep revelations received from her loving Father in Heaven. Now you are holding in your hands what is more than a personal story. This is a deep revelation of the love of God for mankind.

For me it was an inspiration and encouragement for my own ministry around the world. God is so good all the time. My prayer is that you will be blessed just as I was by the reading of this incredible book. Your life will never be the same.

Prophet Louis R. Melo
Louis Melo Ministries
www.melominarchives.org

Peggy takes us on a close up ride with the Father as she holds our hand through her personal experiences. This book is like holding hands with a friend while having tea and sharing how good God is. Each page is an encouragement to rest in the Truth of Scripture and come close to the God who loves us so!

J.E. Berry - Author/Speaker/Singer-Songwriter
(Author of "The Truth About Happiness")
JEBerrySpeaks.com

Peggy McCoy's book is a Holy Spirit filled book. I have known Peggy for over 10 years and her writings have inspired, changed and touched many for God's glory.

Bishop Cleophas Barasa Makona
Return To Jesus Christ Mission, Africa (Kenya)

Dedication

This book is dedicated to my sister Kathy, who passed from this earth into the presence of God far sooner than we wanted. Thank you for sharing with me the depths of your walk with Christ in those final months of your life and inspiring me to crave intimacy of soul with the Lord in a far more personal way than I knew possible. I miss you terribly, and I long for the day when I will see you again in paradise.

Special Thanks

To my Abba Father God
for Your eternal love and mercy.

To my husband Don and best friend,
for your unwavering love and support.

To my precious friends who have
encouraged me to write and tell my story.

To those who have prayed for me for so many years.

CONTENTS

Introduction	....	xv
Chapter 1	Seeking God............................	1
Chapter 2	True Faith Is Believing God	11
Chapter 3	The Amazing Life God Has For Us.........	17
Chapter 4	The Mercy of God......................	22
Chapter 5	The Healing Love of God	29
Chapter 6	Being Still and Listening for His Voice	34
Chapter 7	Holding On to Hope	41
Chapter 8	Life in the Shadow of Death	47
Chapter 9	The Authority of God....................	54
Chapter 10	How Well Do We Know God?.............	60
Chapter 11	God's Joyous Love for Us................	67
Chapter 12	When We Whisper His Name..............	72
Chapter 13	God Does Not Change	77
Chapter 14	The Power of God......................	83
Chapter 15	Humility of Soul........................	88
Chapter 16	The Value of Struggles	92
Chapter 17	God in the Little Things..................	98
Chapter 18	The Peace of God......................	103
Chapter 19	Forgiveness and Growing in Faith	108

Chapter 20	The Rest of God 115
Chapter 21	Monitoring My Thought Life 119
Chapter 22	When Faith is Weary. 126
Chapter 23	The Light of God. 134
Chapter 24	The Power of Rejecting Lies and Embracing God's Truth. 139
Chapter 25	The Blessing of Believing God 146
Chapter 26	Carrying Another's Burden 152
Chapter 27	Holy Week. 159
Chapter 28	God's Peace in the Season of Grieving 165
Chapter 29	What Does It Mean to Really Believe God? . 172
Chapter 30	When God Sings. 178
Chapter 31	A Call to Awaken. 185

Conclusion: The Time To Believe Is Now 192

Introduction

The year was 2002, one of the hardest years of my life. My mother was seventy-eight and dying of cancer. The depth of my grieving was affecting me physically. For two months I had been quite sick, yet the doctors could find nothing wrong with me. Looking back, I believe the stress of not being confident in my mother's eternal salvation was too much for my soul to bear. I prayed and cried out to God with a desperation I had never known before. My mom and I had had many conversations over the years about our faith, and though she knew "about" God and was devout in her Catholic faith, she didn't *know* God, meaning she had not had a personal relationship with Him.

A week before my mom passed away, I sat by her bed talking to her. I felt compelled to sing to her the simple Sunday school song by Anna Bartlett Warner titled "Jesus Loves Me":

> "Jesus loves me! This I know, for the Bible tells me so;
> little ones to Him belong. They are weak but He is strong!

Yes, Jesus loves me! Yes, Jesus loves me!
Yes, Jesus loves me, the Bible tells me so."

Strangely, of all the songs I knew, this was the only one I could remember the words to sing to her. This continued over the next two days.

As I sat with her the following Sunday, I sensed that something significant had changed in her. She was very weak, in immense pain, and now could only talk a little bit at a time, but now she had a light in her eyes that had never been there before. My sister Kathy also noticed this and commented to me about it. I somehow knew she was at peace with God. I suspect God knew she needed to be reminded of the simplicity of childlike faith through that little song. My mom was not one whom I would have ever described as being a joyful person, but that day, her joy was evident to us.

Later that week on Wednesday, my niece Denise was visiting with my mom, telling her of the many things going on that week, although Mom was not conscious at that point. Getting up to leave, my niece said goodbye to her. Suddenly, my mom sat straight up in bed, fully alert and conscious, and said, "Take care of yourself dear." Surprised, she replied, "You take care of yourself too." My mom responded, "I'll be quite fine very shortly." Then she lay back on the pillow,

Introduction

unconscious again. When my niece shared what happened, we all were stunned. That Saturday, Mom died.

On the day of Mom's death, I was resting at a friend's house, exhausted from crying and lack of sleep—grateful her battle was over. Suddenly, I heard my mom's voice so clearly that my eyes flew open—but of course she was not there. I heard her say, "It is so beautiful here!" The Spirit of God then whispered to my soul, "Her joy is full." It was at that moment I knew my mom was in heaven with Jesus. I was overwhelmed with awe, peace, and gratitude.

I later discovered that Psalm 16:11 declares, "You make known to me the path of life; You will fill me with joy in Your presence, with eternal pleasures at Your right hand." And in John 15:11, Jesus said, "These things I have spoken to you, that My joy may remain in you, and that your joy may be full" (NKJV).

I don't know why God granted me such a unique gift as I had just experienced, but I sensed it was to enable me to be at peace and not worry about my mom's eternal home. I had never experienced anything like that before and never since. That event gave me a new intensity of spiritual hunger for God that changed my life forever. It also greatly encouraged my dad and my entire family as we all pondered what happened. I believe that God allowed that experience to thrust me into a more personal and acute awareness that God is really real and He does not want us to fulfill our spiritual hunger just through a religion or busy activities; He wants a vibrant and living relationship with each one of us.

This book is a glimpse into my personal journey in knowing God more intimately and learning to walk out my faith and grow in my knowledge of Jesus Christ, the promised One, as I endeavor to saturate myself with the holy Scriptures, the Bible. My relationship with God has often surprised me. He reveals Himself in the Scriptures and teaches me countless lessons through life events and the people He brings into my life. Most surprisingly, He teaches me how to cultivate a listening heart that is eager to know Him more personally—especially since that year my mom died.

Excerpts from my journals—my prayers, ponderings of what I was dealing with, and how learning to walk with God has impacted my life—are included in the following pages. Some of the entries are what I refer to as God's love letters and "downloads" from heaven. The topics I have chosen to write about are aspects of God's love, character, and some lessons I have learned along my journey so far. Foundationally, I believe the Holy Bible is the Word of God, and any perceived 'letters from heaven' must align with it.

Introduction

I hope you are encouraged as I share a few highlights of my journey. I included blank pages titled 'Reflections' at the end of each chapter should you desire to capture your own ponderings or any thoughts God may impress upon you to contemplate. My earnest prayer is that God will awaken within you an insatiable hunger for His presence, His Word, and His life in you. By His grace may the words in this little book plant and water seeds of faith in your soul so that your joy will also be full!

In my spirit, I sensed the Lord say,

> Beautiful!
> Wonderful!
> Perfect Light!
> Gracious and kind—much delight.
> So at peace in arms of love,
> Protected perfectly from above!
> Freedom in Christ is all you need.
> Don't fight so hard to just succeed.
> My gifts are pure.
> My gifts are free.
> Remember, Beloved,
> The Gift is Me!

Chapter 1
SEEKING GOD

Incline your ear, and come to Me; hear, that your soul may live. (Isaiah 55:3a, ESV)

Over the years since my mom died, I have found that as I earnestly seek God, He graciously meets me. Prior to her passing I didn't know it was possible to have an actual conversation with God, but I have since learned that it is possible for those who truly yearn to hear Him speak. For years I *talked* to God a lot, but I rarely *listened* to Him.

From childhood I was taught about God, but I had no understanding that He wanted a personal relationship with each of us. This began to change late in my senior year of high school while I was participating in a spiritual retreat at my school. I had been struggling with a very unhealthy relationship with a long-time boyfriend. During the retreat, about twenty of us students had quiet time in which we each were to silently pray and rest in God's presence.

Perhaps it was a dream, but as I reclined with my eyes closed, praying to God for direction, I found myself walking on a path through a pretty garden. Ahead of me was my boyfriend calling out to me. I felt unsettled, and I stopped. I turned and saw Jesus on the path going the opposite direction. He turned to me and gently motioned for me to follow Him. I felt overwhelmed with peace and instinctively knew I had to follow Jesus. I began to follow Him as the taunting words of my boyfriend faded behind me.

A few months later I began dating a precious young man who ultimately introduced me to the reality that God made a way for us to have a personal relationship with Him through His Son Jesus. Late one fall evening in 1979, I was all alone and asked Jesus to be my Lord and Savior. This began a new chapter in my spiritual journey. For over a year I went to 5:00 P.M. Catholic Mass on Saturday and then went to a Pentecostal service on Sunday morning. I was trying to figure out who I was becoming in my faith. I had gone to Catholic Mass since I was born, but I found such joy and life at my new church as I heard the Word of God preached in a way that awakened my spirit. I ultimately chose the Pentecostal service as my church home.

In those early years, I grew in my faith and slowly increased my biblical knowledge by reading the Bible and books about the Bible and attending Bible studies off and on. Like all new believers, I made many mistakes along the way as I learned to navigate the often bumpy and winding paths of my life.

Most of my poor choices early on were because I was immature and did not know God's Word of truth, and I had a rebellious spirit; I wanted to do things my way and on my terms, not His. For the first ten years of my Christian walk, I handled the Bible like it was a salad bar: I picked which Scriptures I liked best and focused on them, disregarding the rest. This resulted in a few massive, personal failures in my walk with Christ. Thankfully, He used my failures and backslidings to teach me His mercy. I learned the good news that God loves us so much that He will not leave us as we are, stuck in lies and deceptions.

As I continued the journey through the many chapters of my life, I became increasingly more deliberate in choosing to learn God's Word and submit to His ways. He faithfully began to dismantle the wrong thinking I had become entrenched in. God used numerous biblically grounded pastors, teachers, speakers, friends, and books to teach me the truth from His Word. It has been a miraculous journey, especially the last sixteen years since I have learned to listen more closely to what God has to say and do my best to believe Him.

> "Then you will call upon me and come and pray to me, and I will listen to you. You will seek Me and find Me when you seek Me with all your heart. I will be found by you," declares the Lord. (Jeremiah 29:12–14a)

When it was clear to me that my mom was dying that spring of 2002, I was regularly crying out to God that He would heal her and save her soul. One night I was reading a book on the Christian spiritual life. I was earnestly *wanting* to hear from God. Suddenly, I was surprised by a vivid thought passing through my mind: "You are not prepared for the battle that is before you." Somehow, I was completely aware it was God putting this thought in my mind, and the words scared me to the core. I thought, "What do You mean I am not prepared, and what battle?"

I would come to understand that God was referring to the spiritual battle—God's way versus my way and God's truth versus the lies of the devil, the enemy of our souls. The brief experience that night started yet another chapter in my walk with Jesus. Over the next few years I began praying like I never had before, reading the Bible with heightened interest and a deep belief that God would actually teach me what I needed to know to be prepared for this spiritual battle and to live victoriously. The results have astounded and continue to astound and delight me to the depths of my being.

When I was much younger, I wrote many poems about my faith and my life. I was grateful that God enabled me to express my thoughts in that way. I often wrote God letters and expressed my heart's yearnings in my journals. But gradually I stopped writing as my life became too busy—busy living my life my way, so often just wanting to please other people to "fit in" and habitually working long hours. However, in the past eighteen years, my perspective on the frailty of life has heightened with the death of my parents, a sister, a brother, and many loved ones and friends. This has made me become more introspective, more aware of our eternal souls. Our lives on planet Earth are short—some far shorter than they should be—and I have found solace again in journaling.

There have been a few remarkable interactions with friends and sometimes strangers who spoke to me about things which only God and I knew about. Sometimes these words were of times yet to come in my life. The reality of God's presence became increasingly evident to me. The more time I spent writing my thoughts and prayers, the more I became aware of the Lord encouraging me to write. I learned to listen more carefully and write down what I felt God was saying to me. There have been a multitude of times I have been compelled in my spirit to write paragraphs and sometimes pages of flowing thoughts, thoughts I can hardly keep up with at times. In the beginning it overwhelmed me. I then understood these times to be sacred, overshadowing all else. I increasingly felt immense responsibility concerning this blessing being poured through me. Most times it was clear to me that the Spirit of God was compelling me to write, but I was not sure what I was supposed to do with what was being given to me. It has been an exceedingly sacred matter to me, so I shared with very few what was happening in my quiet time with The Lord.

However, in 2004 I decided to speak to my pastor about all this and shared some of the writings from my journal. After we prayed together, he encouraged me to continue to write and study the Bible prayerfully. He reminded me that the Lord God will never do or say anything that is not in alignment with His written word, the Bible. Those were the best words of advice I could have received. I began to strive to stay in God's Word, reading it regularly. I am still deeply humbled by this remarkable gift God has granted me as I draw near and stay near to Him.

As I endeavor to draw near and stay near to God, I often read books about learning to walk closer with God, learning to hear from God, and I study the Scriptures to grasp the wondrous gift of His Spirit given to those who receive Jesus as their Lord and Savior. In late 2004 I read a book which significantly impacted my walk with God called *The Purpose Driven Life* by Rick Warren. It helped me better grasp what God created me for. Another book that blessed me was *Hungry for God* by Margaret Feinberg. In it she expounds on the various ways God communicates with us and how critical it is to use the Holy Bible to gauge whether we are truly hearing from God. I often need the wisdom of others, so I stay on the lookout for great books that will help me mature in my faith.

But more than any others, I treasure the words of Jesus Christ. In John 16:7–14, He teaches His disciples that the Holy Spirit is the Spirit of Truth and will always bring glory to Jesus.

> [Jesus said to his disciples] "If you love me, keep my commands. And I will ask the Father, and he will give you another advocate to help you and be with you forever–the Spirit of truth. The world cannot accept him, because it neither sees him nor knows him. But you know him, for he lives with you and will be in you. All this I have spoken while still with you. But the Advocate, the Holy Spirit, whom the Father will send in my name, will teach you all things and will remind

you of everything I have said to you." (John 14:15–17, 25–26)

What no eye has seen, what no ear has heard, and what no human mind has conceived—the things God has prepared for those who love him—these are the things God has revealed to us by his Spirit. The Spirit searches all things, even the deep things of God. For who knows a person's thoughts except their own spirit within them? In the same way no one knows the thoughts of God except the Spirit of God. What we have received is not the spirit of the world, but the Spirit who is from God, so that we may understand what God has freely given us. This is what we speak, not in words taught us by human wisdom but in words taught by the Spirit, explaining spiritual realities with Spirit-taught words. (1 Corinthians 2:9–13)

For years I have felt strongly that others would be encouraged by many of the entries that fill my journals. I have shared passages with friends who then expressed how important it was that I continue to write. Recently, God has been strongly urging me to write this book so that everyone could know how close

SEEKING GOD

He is, how real He is, and how profound His love for each one of us is.

God knows we need constant encouragement and strengthening in our faith walk with Jesus. He has surprised me with His faithful provision to meet my every need, even needs I didn't know I would have. I have found that most people are like me, needing encouragement and strengthening daily because, as a dear friend of mine says, "Life down here on Earth is hard."

My prayer is that you would know intimacy of soul with God our Creator—intimacy which I have come to rely on—and enjoy beyond what words could express. I also encourage you to open the Bible every day, read, and fervently seek God so that you will know Him more and more each day of your life. He is the Lord God of all creation. He is real, He lives, and He loves each of us with a perfect, eternal, and astounding love. Yes, God loves *you* this way.

> Write down for the coming generation what the Lord has done, so that people not yet born will praise Him. (Psalm 102:18 GNT)

Reflections

Chapter 2:
TRUE FAITH IS BELIEVING GOD

> These are written that you may believe that Jesus is the Messiah, the Son of God, and that by believing you may have life in his name. (John 20:31)

I am so grateful that my parents raised me in the knowledge that there is a God to whom I am accountable. As a child, I thought He lived at my church. Of course, this did not prevent me from doing things I knew could get me into trouble! As I became a young adult, I learned that faith was more than believing there is a God and that He was so much bigger than I had ever imagined. James 2:19 says that even the demons believe there is one God—and shudder. So what is the importance of faith *in* God? It is clearly more than simply believing He exists.

My life journey has been moving from believing there is a God, to knowing about Him and casually reading the

Bible, and then to grasping the depth of the Scriptures, the true purpose and power of faith—which is to believe God, know Him, love Him, and serve Him.

Romans 4:16 refers to Abraham as the father of our faith. He believed God and God called him His friend. I find this amazing: being God's friend is possible! God spoke to him about many things and promised him many descendants, and because Abraham believed what God said, it was accounted to him for righteousness; his faith made him right with God (James 2:23–24).

In my quiet time with the Lord, it is usually my habit to listen to, or read the Scriptures and talk with Him about it. I often ask God what a verse or chapter means and how I am to apply it to my life. Sometimes I don't sense an answer, so I will study more on the topic, pray for insight, and ask trusted advisors who love God's Word. Other times I gain a new understanding. I tell God my needs and pray about many things. I often journal about my concerns, thoughts, hopes, prayers, and what I believe the Lord is saying to me. Occasionally I strongly sense I *must* write. I cannot explain it other than to say I hear the words in my spirit. At times it is like a whisper, and other times it is with such power that my eyes well with tears, and I am washed with reverent awe.

True Faith Is Believing God

I am increasingly encouraged in my heart that God wants me to simply believe Him—to know His Word, believe His Word, and love His Word. As often as He has told me this, I still don't believe Him as much as I think I do or as much as He wants me to. I say this because of how regularly He asks me to just believe Him. God teaches throughout His Word about how important it is that we believe Him and not doubt Him:

> "You are my witnesses," declares the Lord, "and my servant whom I have chosen, so that you may know and believe me and understand that I am he. Before me no god was formed, nor will there be one after me. I, even I, am the Lord, and apart from me there is no savior." (Isaiah 43:10-11)

Jesus said, "Very truly I tell you, whoever hears my word and believes him who sent me has eternal life and will not be judged but has crossed over from death to life" (John 5:24).

When speaking of Jesus, the apostle Peter said, "All the prophets testify about him that everyone who believes in him receives forgiveness of sins through his name" (Acts 10:43).

I believe that doubt and unbelief is the opposite of faith. This does not mean that those who love God do not struggle with doubt. I often do, but I have learned that if I feed my faith, my doubt will starve to death, and the opposite is likewise true.

The Bible is full of wisdom, instruction, promises, and revelations. It is also full of extraordinary stories of how God continually revealed Himself to peoples and individuals, clearly stating what He required of them and how deeply He loved them. He was always clear about the abundant blessings of obedience to His ways and the disastrous consequences of rebellion against them. I increasingly want to please God in all that I think, say, and do, though I do not always succeed. This is why I rely on His mercy.

Hebrews 11:6 says that without faith it is impossible to please God. So, with faith in Him we actually make Him happy. This is a surprising truth to me. Jesus often stated that the miracles He did were in direct correlation to the faith of the person crying out to Him. In some towns Jesus did only a few miracles because of their lack of faith, and this grieved him (Matthew 13:58).

As I was praying and journaling one day, I was compelled to write the following:

True Faith Is Believing God

Believe, Beloved. Believe My Words of promise revealed in the Bible. Believe Me. This is the foundation of your spiritual house. With faith anything is possible as you stand in Jesus Christ and seek to honor Me in all things. The salvation of souls is the most critical thing. For the greater good I give you these words to strengthen My church and increase the faith of many, for holiness and purity in the followers of Christ. I desire this for all of My children. Tell them I love them. Tell them I live!

To all who did receive him (Jesus), to those who believed in his name, he gave the right to become children of God. (John 1:12)

Reflections

Chapter 3
The Amazing Life God Has for Us

[Jesus said] I have come that they may have life, and that they may have it more abundantly. (John 10:10b, NKJV)

God is the source of all life. Many do not contemplate the depth and power of this truth. For those who love God Almighty and have received the gift of the life of His Son Jesus the Christ, they have at their fingertips "abundant life." But do we grasp this life with both hands and pull it into our chest and make it our daily strength?

When I was seventeen, I learned I could have a personal relationship with God because of what Jesus did for me. I did not grasp the immensity of the decision, but I chose to accept Jesus as my Lord and Savior because I realized I needed help that only He could provide and I wanted to be in right relationship with God. However, for many years after that, I did not walk in the strength of Christ's abundant life. I often struggled with understanding "why not?"

I have come to believe it was because I wanted to be a Christian on my terms. I thought I was being faithful to live for Jesus, and in many ways I suppose I was. I read the Bible from time to time. I went to church. But in retrospect, "I" was most often the central part of the equation. I am so grateful that God is merciful, patient, gracious, and kind. Like a little child learns how to crawl, sit up, walk, and then run, so do we grow and learn in our relationship with God. We fall and get up and try again. Growing in Christ is a lifelong process, and God faithfully stays very near as we learn to walk with Him. Even in the seasons we neglect Him, He stays closer than the air we breathe.

The Bible is clear that we all are tempted to sin, which is anything contrary to God's ways. However, 1 Corinthians 10:13 says that God makes a way of escape for us each time we are faced with the temptation to sin in any way, but we each must choose to turn away from the temptation. Many times in my life I did not choose the escape route because I was naïve, deceived, or believed that I just had to *do* or *have* something to be happy. Often the way of escape is a thought telling us to not do that thing or to get out of that place or situation. Sometimes it is a friend who expresses concern. Our natural thoughts say, "If God loves me then He would want me to be happy." But does a loving mother or father always let their child do whatever the child thinks will make them happy? Absolutely not!

A loving parent must say no to their child many times and try to stop certain behaviors because they have the wisdom and life experience to know that many things that look quite fun and innocent to a child are actually not good for them at all. God loves us far more than any earthly parent could ever love their child, and God's wisdom is so much greater than mankind's wisdom. I have learned that when God's Word says something is harmful to us, it really is harmful long term. When God says something is evil, it truly is even if we don't understand why.

We can choose to learn from other people's mistakes or from our own poor choices. It sure is far less painful to learn from other's mistakes! Better yet, we can learn from obedience. I love that the Bible is full of hundreds of real-life stories of people's good and bad choices in how they lived and how they did or did not walk with God. The more time I spend reading the Bible, the more I see how we are the same today as those people who lived so long ago: stubborn and prideful and wanting to be self-sufficient, often calling on God only when we are desperate.

The amazing life that God has for us is far more than just living and breathing. It is learning to walk humbly with our God, learning how to do what is right in His eyes and enjoying abundant life. It is discovering the joy of intimacy of soul with the Creator of the universe and being amazed daily at His great love for us.

> For God so loved the world that He gave His one and only Son, that whoever believes in him shall not perish but have eternal life. For God did not send His Son into the world to condemn the world, but to save the world through him. (John 3:16–17)

The longer I walk with God, the more this truth astounds me. I urge you to stop and consider what this verse means. Take the time to do this; it will be time well spent. Even if you have called yourself a Christian for a long time, pause and reflect on how profound this gift is.

Reflections

Chapter 4
THE MERCY OF GOD

> Because of His great love for us, God, who is rich in mercy, made us alive with Christ even when we were dead in transgressions—it is by grace you have been saved. (Ephesians 2:4–5)

God is perfect; we are not. The love of God is holy and pure, and He is unashamed to call us His own. The implications of this are startling. I have often considered the magnitude of it.

Although it has not always been the case in my life, more recently there are times when I think I am doing a pretty good job of living a life that would honor God. This is now my life goal. I desire to please the Lord in the way I behave, think, speak, work, play, rest, and dream.

Then I do something foolish. It may be a prideful and judgmental attitude concerning someone who crosses my path, or I might just do something outright dumb or say something senseless without thinking first. I may not do something the Lord has instructed me in my heart to do, like writing an encouraging note or calling a friend I keep thinking about. Sometimes it takes me hours, days, or even weeks to figure out that I am out of alignment with Him.

Busyness is a great mechanism to distract me from settling down and listening to His still, small voice within my soul. Sometimes my first inclination is to feel guilty, and then I delay thinking about or talking to Him about the matter. My pride can cause me to avoid Him. Have you ever done that? You are guilty of something—maybe something big, maybe something quite small—but you don't want to face up to it or be held accountable. The old selfish nature within us rears its ugly head, and we choose to stay at a distance from our God. I have often done that. Other times I notice immediately, and in my heart I tell Him I am sorry, and I thank Him for His immense grace and tender love. I am then reunited with His merciful heart, at peace again.

I have learned that it pleases God a great deal when I quickly turn to Him, turning away from my pride. This attitude and behavior shows Him that I believe Him. It is my deepest desire to pay attention to my heart attitude at all times so that I am quick to adjust the direction of my thoughts and realign myself with His heart. The wonderful benefit of this choice is that I am at peace in my heart, mind, and soul, staying in fellowship with God. It is possible to minimize the barriers to receiving the expanse of His great love, the hindrances to experiencing the fullness of joy He pours out. It is all about bringing every thought to Jesus and embracing His Word.

Why do we so often think we have to have it all together before we can draw near to God? Romans 5:8 tells us that God demonstrates His own love for us in this: While we were still sinners, Christ died for us. This truth means we should not wait to run to His arms of grace.

> What, then, shall we say in response to this? If God is for us, who can be against us? He who did not spare His own Son, but gave Him up for us all—how will He not also, along with Him, graciously give us all things? Who will bring any charge against those whom God has chosen? It is God who justifies. Who then is he that condemns? No one.
>
> Christ Jesus, who died—more than that, who was raised to life—is at the right hand of God and is also interceding for us.

> Who shall separate us from the love of Christ? Shall trouble or hardship or persecution or famine or nakedness or danger or sword? . . . No, in all these things we are more than conquerors through Him who loved us. For I am convinced that neither death nor life, neither angels nor demons, neither the present nor the future, nor any powers, neither height nor depth, nor anything else in all creation, will be able to separate us from the love of God that is in Christ Jesus our Lord. (Romans 8:31–35, 37–39)

As I sit here contemplating these things, I find myself basking in the greatness of God's love for all of us. He is faithful to teach us how to have a relationship with Him if only we truly desire this, and He rewards our tiny acts of obedience for the sake of the honor of His name.

> He leads me in the paths of righteousness
> for His name's sake. (Psalm 23:3 ESV)

There are dozens of stories in the Bible about real people who tried all sorts of ways to serve God other than what He instructed. Some ended tragically. Yet Micah 6:8 states the simplicity of it:

> He has shown you, O mortal, what is good. And what does the Lord require of you? To act justly and to love mercy and to walk humbly with your God.

I particularly love the stories in the Bible about King David. He loved the Lord and diligently sought to serve and please God in all matters, but like me, he was not always successful in his efforts.

Like we often do, there were times he became complacent and prideful and did some terrible and foolish things that had consequences he, his family, and his nation had to live with. Yet God, in His extravagant love and mercy, immediately restored relationship with David each time he came to his senses and turned to God in humility and repentance. Even with all of David's imperfections, God said of him, "I have found in David son of Jesse, a man after My heart, who will do all My will" (Acts 13:22, ESV). Now that is a compliment I yearn to receive from the Creator of the universe!

The year my mom died I read a compelling book titled *The Diary of Sister Maria Faustina, Divine Mercy in my Soul.* What surprised and delighted me was reading about how regularly she heard from God in her prayer time. This set my heart on a journey of grasping God's mercy and love more intently. For many years my failures kept me from walking boldly in my faith. I am now finding that the more I grasp God's mercy, the more bold I become. I have come to rely on God's promise, "There is now no condemnation for those who are in Christ Jesus (Romans 8:1). The older I get, the more acutely aware of God's mercy I become—both my need for it and the abundance of it I find as I rest in God's presence.

A prayer rises up within me: "Help me to turn quickly to You each day Lord. Help me love You more than I do. I want to know You more than I do. Help me love Your Word and understand it more each day."

> [Jesus said] My sheep listen to my voice; I know them, and they follow me. (John 10:27)

Reflections

Chapter 5
THE HEALING LOVE OF GOD

> The Lord is close to the brokenhearted and saves those who are crushed in spirit. (Psalm 34:18)

There are times when we all need the reassurance that we are loved and accepted. For much of my life I struggled with feelings of not being good enough, feeling the need to please other people, sometimes to my own detriment. In my walk with God, I also often struggled, wondering whether God really loved the mess I often am.

One particular year I had been stumbling through a hard season in my life. I was grieving the recent death of a loved one, overwhelmed with changes in my job, and had been inconsistent in my walk with Christ. Then someone dear to me misunderstood something I had done and ended their relationship with me. I was heartbroken.

Many times in my weariness and in seasons of grief, I find a quiet place to pray and cry out to God for help and relief. He faithfully gathers me into His arms to wipe away my tears. It was during that tear-filled time the Lord gave me yet another beautiful love letter that encouraged me and soothed my soul. I have come to believe that these letters can encourage many others too. His words bring the comfort, healing, and perspective we continually need.

I heard in my spirit, "Write." I sat down to capture the thoughts that came flooding into my mind:

> I love you with an everlasting and powerful love. My love is not dependent on how strong you are; it is dependent only on My faithfulness to My Word, which is forever true and cannot be changed.
>
> I love you with a perfect, never-ending, unfailing love. I do not love as mankind loves, with impure motives, judgments, and doubt. My love never wavers. There is nothing that you could do to make Me stop loving you. Believe My words, which are true.
>
> Do your best each day, and do not worry so! You act as if I cannot or will not do

all I have promised. Rejoice in My faithfulness and unfailing love.

Walk in power and confidence today. Grasp this truth: Christ is in you, the hope of glory. This is your righteousness before Me. Not your faithfulness—but Mine. Yes, I long for you to walk faithfully before Me in Christ, but you must not get so discouraged by your weaknesses and human frailties. Rejoice in your weaknesses, for in your weakness I am strong and demonstrate My glory.

At the cross of Christ take up My robe of perfection and righteousness. There, find your peace, your hope, and your glory. I have all the answers to all your questions, but I would prefer you just trust Me, believe Me, and count on Me to be there in every moment of need, in every moment of rest, in every moment of abundance and joy, in every struggle, and in each moment of suffering. All of this will bring Me glory. For it is in the everyday activities and realities that I prove My power, glory, and authority over the evil one and sin.

Rest therefore in My strong and capable arms of grace. My mercy is sufficient for you, dear child. Instead of worrying, pray. Worry wastes time and drains you of your strength. Remember that apart from Me you can do nothing. That means you need Christ Jesus, for everything! Yes, even to pray, to be faithful, and to walk uprightly before Me. I only desire you believe Me, trust Me, and take Me at My word.

My mercy is your perfect covering. Your purpose is in Me and for Me. Remember who I am. Focus on Me. Be singularly focused and devoted to Me. I am the one who fulfills My purpose in you and through you. I only require a humble and contrite heart—one that is fully submitted to Me, to My perfect will. I will provide all you need. Trust Me.

Praise be to the God and Father of our Lord Jesus Christ, the Father of compassion and the God of all comfort. (2 Corinthians 1:3)

Reflections

Chapter 6
BEING STILL AND LISTENING FOR HIS VOICE

> Come to me, all you who are weary and burdened, and I will give you rest. (Matthew 11:28)

When the Lord speaks to my soul, most of the time it is hard to convince myself that it is anything other than the Spirit of God. But sometimes I dismiss the whispered words that gently draw me to Him. Sometimes in my busyness I just ignore what I hear in my heart. Other times, I long so much to just rest in His presence that I finally mute my phone, turn off the TV, decide not to fuss with everything beckoning to be done, and intentionally still myself. I open my Bible to read and pray.

Psalm 46:10 tells us, "Be still, and know that I am God." In this crazy, busy world, I know of no other invitation that is so full of life, peace, and rest for my soul. Sometimes I put on my calendar, "Spend time with God." I want to intentionally choose to be content with being still and quiet before Him. I put everything else on my calendar and to-do list, so why not the most important thing?

Yet, I get frustrated with myself sometimes. Why is it so hard to do something so wondrously beneficial and restful, something I enjoy so much? Like most people, I get distracted by the noise and chaos of the world, the never-ending list of things I need or want to do. Tragedies and natural disasters bring anxiety, and the health crises of loved ones cause such distress. There is also the relentless sway of the world to believe lies to keep me focused on anything but Jesus. Sometimes it feels like too much effort to 'be still' and hide myself in Christ. There are times it *seems* easier to just mentally shut down and turn on the TV. However, the truth is that in God's presence we find peace and power to balance the craziness of our lives, to live the life of purpose that God intended for us to live, and to overcome the deceptions of the world and the enemy of our soul.

On one of those days when I felt overwhelmed and weary, I sat down with my Bible as an act of obedience to be still. After some time, the Lord whispered in my heart, "Write."

> I alone am God. There is no other. The
> devil deceives the multitudes, but My

people know the truth, for they know My Word. Stay in My Word so that you will have the protection you need from his lies. Stand firm and listen always for My voice. I am always revealing myself to My creation, but so few desire to know Me, so they look away and entertain themselves with useless activities that have no eternal value.

You are to pray for my people, dear one. They may know about Me, but they do not know Me as I desire they know Me. I created mankind to walk humbly with Me, to love mercy and to do what is just and right at all times. I created mankind to have fellowship with Me, to learn to love righteousness, and to be transformed into the image of My beloved Son Jesus—He is your model to imitate.

You are to fear nothing. My Spirit is the Spirit of love, power, and a sound mind. The enemy brings doubt, fear, confusion, and death. I bring life. The battle for souls is great; do not be deceived. But I am greater than the enemy. Of this you can be confident and bold.

So many of My people, My children, are like empty cups on a shelf. They are not being used for their purpose. They are cups upside down, empty of Me and dusty from lack of use. Pray they would turn to Me and cleanse themselves with the water of My Word. Then I can fill them, and they can be used to refresh the souls of the lost and weary. A cup is meant to be used, to be poured out.

Just as a candle that is not lit cannot shine, so are My people who are not filled with the light of My Word. Pray that My church would hunger for My light and to be filled with My Spirit; then they will be useable vessels in My hands. Only then can I fulfill the purpose for which I created them.

I am the Lord God of all creation; hear My words of truth! My Word, the Bible, is the truth. Humbly come before Me and ask Me to instruct you in the ways of prayer, and the power of My Spirit will lead you as you fill yourself with Me by praying in Christ's name. I will indeed teach you all you need to know, and I will be your power, wisdom, and peace, for apart from Me you can do nothing.

Pray for My blessings to be poured out on the earth. Devote yourself to prayer with joy. I await you each day to meet with Me. Do not pass Me by in your busyness. I multiply your time, energy, and capacity for knowledge.

Humility is the starting place, the door that opens up to My children both My power and My blessings. All authority is Mine, and I give you the power you need. But this power is dependent on you spending time with Me and in My Word and you asking Me daily to fill you and lead you by My Spirit to protect you from the evil one.

Tell My people the Bible still is My primary way of speaking to My people, to all who seek Me. My Spirit speaks words of revelation and insights as you stay near to Me and desire to hear My voice. So many of My children do not desire to hear My voice—they have believed the lie that I no longer speak. It should not be so. It wounds My heart that so many of My children think I stopped speaking and communing with My people when Jesus ascended to Heaven to take His rightful place at My side. But did I not send My Holy Spirit to continue what Jesus began? Yes! The Spirit reveals and speaks and comforts—from that day until Christ returns as King of kings. Grieve not My Spirit by rejecting His gifts or by resisting the fruit of My Spirit. Receive the fullness of all I pour out into the church through My Spirit and My Word—they are one.

I will instruct you and teach you in the way you should go; I will counsel you with my loving eye on you. (Psalm 32:8)

Reflections

Chapter 7
Holding On to Hope

> Now hope does not disappoint, because
> the love of God has been poured out in
> our hearts by the Holy Spirit who was
> given to us. (Romans 5:5)

Have you ever had a tremendously difficult season in your life where it seems everything that could go wrong does, and then some? I know you have, as I have, and it tests our faith to the very core of our being. Like you, I have had times I have been so discouraged that I can't pray—or times I don't want to pray because it will expose how upset I am at God for allowing such hardship to suffocate me or my loved ones.

When I have no strength to hope anymore, when it seems I have no faith left, this is when I am face to face with how small I am and why Christ died to save us. This is when I realize how completely and utterly I am dependent on God, not just for my salvation, my breath, and heartbeat, but even for my faith in Him. Empty of myself, with no tears left to cry, exhausted from trying to do everything I know to do, I whisper the only prayer that is left: "Help me, Jesus."

When I whisper that simple prayer, I believe it is evidence that someone is praying for me. It may be a friend responding to the Holy Spirit, who brought me to their mind. The Bible tells us that Christ Himself intercedes for us before the Father (Hebrews 7:25). Romans 8:26–27 proclaims another profound truth about The Holy Spirit:

> The Spirit helps us in our weakness. We do not know what we ought to pray for, but the Spirit Himself intercedes for us with groans that words cannot express. And He who searches our hearts knows the mind of the Spirit, because the Spirit intercedes for the saints in accordance with God's will.

What an encouragement it is to know that when we can't pray, we can depend on both the Holy Spirit and Jesus to pray for us. Pause and think about this. This is the extravagant love of God for us. This hushes my soul. Also, it is surprising to me that the Bible refers to those who love Jesus and walk with Him as saints, even though we are just redeemed sinners. These things awaken hope within me again and again.

Matthew 5:3 tells us, "Blessed are the poor in spirit, for theirs is the kingdom of heaven." I believe the awareness of our complete and utter dependence on God for everything is what being "poor in spirit" means. Isn't it odd that when we are at our weakest state, God rewards us for our faith?

Since God goes to such lengths to keep us close to Him, is this not a good reason to hold on to our hope in His faithfulness to bring us through the darkest of times? I say yes because I have found time and time again that it is worth it to do so.

In seasons when hardship overwhelms us, this is when all those Scriptures we have read and heard over the years become our lifeline to the truth, reminding us of God's character, His faithfulness, and His love for us. This is when God shows up in a whole new way, resulting in a deeper level of intimacy in our soul as we hold on tight to His promises and choose to believe Him for everything. This is the childlike faith that delights Him.

> And without faith it is impossible to please God, because anyone who comes to Him must believe that He exists and that He rewards those who earnestly seek Him. (Hebrews 11:6)

Written during a particularly rough season of my life, this entry in my journal from the Lord still comforts me:

> Beloved, hope in My promises is powerful and effective in pushing back waves of darkness that the enemy of your soul would like you to drown under. In times of despair you may think you are alone, but you are not. You may feel I have forgotten you, but that is impossible. Your name is inscribed in the palm of My hand, and you are the apple of My eye. Never doubt this truth.
>
> Just because there is pain and disappointments and at times great fear gripping your mind because of the unknown, this does not mean that My love for you has diminished. It is only evidence that you live in a fallen and imperfect world, which is why Jesus was sent to redeem all of creation.
>
> But this world is not all there is. No, you are a citizen of heaven, which is the eternal destination of all who choose Jesus. This is your hope: confidence in My faithfulness to care for My own and to work all things together for good. It

may not seem good to you, but I have a higher perspective, a broader view of the full truth. This is when it is vital to trust Me, Beloved.

Hope in My promises; expect Me to bring beauty from ashes. I am trustworthy. Watch and see what I will do. It will astound you.

Reflections

Chapter 8
Life in the Shadow of Death

> Even though I walk through the valley of
> the shadow of death, I will fear no evil,
> for you are with me. (Psalm 23:4a ESV)

It was a sunny morning in May 2003 when my sister Kathy called me as I was driving to work. She said, "I have pancreatic cancer. The doctors say I have nine months to live."

My whole world stopped. My mind could not grasp what she had said. As she told me more, I pulled to the side of the road to try to process the words she was saying. We cried together.

I remember looking out over Crystal Springs Reservoir, where I was parked, its peaceful waters reflecting the beautiful green trees along the shoreline, and thinking to myself, "How can the world be so beautiful and also so terrible?" It had been only eleven months since my mom had died of cancer, and now this?

In the weeks and months that followed I was on the phone with Kathy almost daily—praying together, crying together, dreaming together, and believing God could heal her but not knowing whether He would. Together we searched the Scriptures for wisdom, comfort, and answers. Her husband Tom took her to the unending stream of doctor appointments and retired early from his job to take care of her and their three precious children. How could life be so unfair? We trusted God to sustain us.

That summer we went on a week-long vacation together through the San Juan Islands in the Pacific Northwest. It was a peaceful and joy-filled week I will treasure forever. Kathy's hair was falling out due to the chemotherapy. She somehow made light of it, and we laughed through our tears. She had a great attitude, and she chose to enjoy each day to the fullest. We both determined to stay close to Jesus in the valley of the shadow of death.

The crazy part of this story is that before Kathy was diagnosed with cancer, I hadn't known she was a Christian. This stunned me. She told me that she had accepted Jesus fifteen years prior. Why hadn't she told me? Why hadn't I spoken more to her about my faith? She and I had not been very close for many years as our lives diverged due to interests and distance. We talked about this, and we both were sad that we were not more expressive and bold in our faith with each other, so we decided to change that and make up for lost time.

Over the following months we became extremely close. Almost every day, she would tell me on the phone all that was going on in her home: the chemo treatments, how lousy she felt some days, how happy she was when she felt good on other days, how the kids and Tom were doing, and the many wonderful friends and neighbors who would visit her and help in so many ways.

Looking back, I think perhaps the greatest gift she gave me during this horrible season was her transparency—raw honesty and vulnerability. She chose to confide in me her dreams, secrets, her darkest thoughts, and also her most sacred experiences with Jesus.

One day in 2004 she was telling me how tired she was from the battle. That morning as she was talking with God, she said that she closed her eyes, crawled up into His lap, and He was rocking her like a little child, telling her how much He loved her and that this world was only her temporary home. She told me she could hear His heartbeat, that she had never felt so loved, so peaceful, and that He answered many of her questions. I listened with intent. It saddened me that I had never had an experience with God like that.

That day ignited a new depth in my walk with God. I wanted to know Him like Kathy had come to know Him. I began praying differently, more honestly, reading the Scriptures with more hunger to know more about this amazing God we serve, and desiring to love and know Him like Kathy had come to love and know Him as she came face to face with her mortality.

Nineteen months after her diagnosis, Kathy went home to be with Jesus. She was forty-nine; we were all devastated. My faith was shaken to the core. I really believed God would heal her, yet she died. I was non-functional for weeks. I was confused—crushed that God would take Kathy away from her three children and her husband, from our families. From me.

About a month after we buried her—a dark month of unanswered questions and more tears than I thought were possible to cry—I begged God to help me make sense of things. I was mad and questioning everything I had heard from God. I then heard Him whisper to me in my spirit, "Will you also leave me?" Without thinking I responded, "Where else am I to go, Lord? You alone have the words of eternal life." This declaration began the slow healing of my heart and brought about a deeper sense of the frailty of life and our need for God's mercy.

LIFE IN THE SHADOW OF DEATH

Over the months that followed I came to grasp that the nearness and love of God transcends our pain and our limited understanding. I learned how He carries us through the valley of the shadow of death and the immensity of life that exists there. The truth that Jesus overcame death and the grave so that we could as well took on new meaning for me and gave me new comfort and strength.

In my desperation and pain, I too learned how to crawl up into my heavenly Father's lap to receive comfort. In my weakness I learned anew how to rely on His strength. It required time alone with God, waiting on Him and listening, holding tightly to His promises. I learned yet again not to trust my own understanding but to continually seek His direction and counsel. I also learned that just because I cannot comprehend God's ways does not mean He is not faithful.

Is there a life lesson to be gleaned from all this? Yes. When there is a person in our life who is struggling, we can come alongside to just be there, love them, and listen to their heart cries. Let's grasp the truth that our presence makes a difference. Our gift to others is to be present and walk the difficult road with them. It does not matter that we don't have all the answers. We can make every second count, acutely aware of the gift of the time we are given each day. The blessing flows both ways. Every conversation is important, regardless how few or how many words are spoken. Sadly, I sometimes forget this truth even to this day.

These many years later I still miss Kathy terribly. I miss the friendship we developed in that intensely difficult season. I have some regrets, but I continue to trust that our faithful God will redeem all that has been lost, all the crushed dreams.

I look forward to seeing her again in paradise. True faith is revealed in the testing. Kathy passed the final test with grace. I pray I will too.

> God shall wipe away all tears from their eyes. There shall be no more death. Neither shall there be any more sorrow nor crying nor pain, for the former things have passed away. (Revelation 21:4 MEV)

Reflections

Chapter 9
THE AUTHORITY OF GOD

> For I am God, and there is no other;
> I am God, and there is none like me,
> declaring the end from the beginning
> and from ancient times things not yet
> done, saying, 'My counsel shall stand,
> and I will accomplish all my purpose.'
> (Isaiah 46:9-10 ESV)

In May 2006 my pastor gave everyone in our small church family a copy of *The One Year Bible*. For the first time in years I seemed to be able to read the Bible almost every day. I learned anew that God wanted me to ask Him my questions about what I read, so I did. Sometimes I would suddenly, clearly understand something that previously was confusing to me. Other times I received no clarity in my alone time with God, so I would talk with my pastor and Christian friends about what I was struggling with.

One day, after reading Matthew chapters 5-7, I had many questions rise up in my mind, and I prayed that

The Authority Of God

God would answer my questions and help me understand His ways. I heard in my heart, "Write."

> The ways of My kingdom are not the ways of the world. They are contrary to man's ways and often seem impossible to the mind of man. The eyes of faith see My power and My kingdom principles. I have authority over all natural laws for I created the universe. I have authority over all in the spirit world for I created all that is seen and unseen.
>
> I am spirit, and I desire you to walk in My ways. It requires obedience to My Word and turning away from the world's ways and your natural thoughts. My Word is power and life. I spoke all things into existence by My word. The touch of My hand is healing for all whom I love. Be aware that there are many types of healing. When I am rejected I will not stay, but where I am honored I can do the miraculous.
>
> I desire that you walk in My kingdom ways, Beloved. But you must grasp My kingdom truths. They are more real than what you see with your eyes. Many do

not believe the stories I have recorded in the Bible, yet they are all true. For those who will believe, My Word is power and life! It is My way to reveal Myself to My creation. It is My desire to be found by all those who seek Me.

My disciple Peter was bold and unruly; he was proud and self-sufficient—a capable businessman and husband. But such a man cannot be used in My kingdom unless he sees his own weaknesses and grasps My authority. Once he came to the end of himself and received My pure love and mercy, My authority, holiness, and power, then I could use him to do great things on earth for My kingdom purposes. Only when he understood his own depravity did he desire My holiness. It was then that I could use him to build My church. He became a great leader because he understood the power of being utterly dependent on Me.

I am Jesus Christ, Son of the most high God. My Father has given Me all authority in heaven and on earth. My ways bring life, power, and salvation to those who receive Me and hunger for

Me. But to those who reject Me, I am foolishness. I will not force Myself on any soul. But it is not My desire that any would perish, which is eternal separation from God's presence in outer darkness and unending despair.

Consider these things and ask for more understanding and wisdom. Pray for spiritual discernment and protection from the enemy, that great liar and deceiver, the devil. I desire you to know My truths, Beloved. Hunger for My kingdom truths!

Be anointed with My oil of refreshing, My water of life, My Spirit of power. Receive what I have released to you, Beloved. For My glory I do this. Proclaim to all that I live, that I, the Lord of Hosts, have delivered all people from the ravages of sin and destruction, if they would only call out to Me, seek Me, and hunger to know Me with intimacy of soul.

Humility before Me is true worship in spirit and truth. Prayer for souls honors Me because it is evidence that you know I died on the cross to save mankind from being eternally separated from God due to their sins.

Grasp My authority over all that exists. Can you? No, but try to. Yes, all things in the heavens and on the earth are under My complete authority. Blessed are those who believe Me and obey My words of life.

Reflections

Chapter 10
HOW WELL DO WE KNOW GOD?

> Now this is eternal life: that they know you, the only true God, and Jesus Christ, whom you have sent. (John 17:3)

This question struck me one day: "How well do you know God?" The thought persistently swirled in my mind.

I wondered, what if there was a scale of one to ten? One on the scale could be "I don't know what the question means because no one can know God." Ten on the scale might be "God is more real to me than the people in this room and all the things I can touch. His presence is all I need to live and breathe and know eternal life, eternal joy, and eternal peace."

Have you ever considered this question? Perhaps you have not thought about this in a very long time. For me, I have been at one on this scale. I have also known God at perhaps eight on this scale. That particular day the question haunted me because I didn't feel I knew God very well. I felt far away from Him. I thought that my knowing God was perhaps a weak five on this imaginary scale of mine.

How could that be? Have you ever been very close to someone and then months or years later you don't know them as well, or perhaps you don't feel you know them at all anymore?

Knowing a person is in direct correlation to the amount of time spent with that person. How often do you talk or hang out together? How often do you listen to the deepest thoughts of their heart, their greatest dreams, hopes, and plans? The questions you ask often reveal how close you are. Taking the time to listen to the full answer is a reflection of the depth of that relationship, even if it takes hours, days, weeks, or years. It can reveal the level of intimacy of soul that exists between the two of you.

It starts with the desire to know a person more than you do. A soul will draw you somehow. Perhaps it is their character, attitude, integrity, or spirit. Something about them intrigues you. Sometimes it is emotional; other times it is intellectual or spiritual. It could be in reaction to a crisis. God draws us to Himself the same way. Are we paying attention?

How often have you said hello to someone, hoping for a short chat but receiving instead a passing, hurried "hello" as they went on their way? I have learned that God says hello to us throughout each day hoping we will stop, say hello back, and talk with Him for a while.

God has written us many letters and recorded many stories in the Bible of His relationship with various people and nations. This is indeed an awe-inspiring book in which the God of all the universe chose to reveal Himself and His ways to mankind. Why would the Creator of all that exists, seen and unseen, reveal Himself to a person, a nation, or the world? It is because God loves us (1 John 4:9–10). But we are rebellious and proud and often dismiss Him. Why would He love us so? I have often contemplated this question.

A mother bears a child and loves that child no matter what. Each of us loves someone—friends, family, or a pet. Why? Because God first loved us!

> Before I formed you in the womb I knew you, before you were born I set you apart. (Jeremiah 1:5)

Yes, before He created us, He knew us and loved us! He gave us the ability to love. The Bible says God so loved the world that He gave His one and only son, Jesus, that whoever believes in Him shall not perish but have eternal life (John 3:16). It also says that the wages of sin is death, but the gift of God is eternal life through Christ Jesus our Lord (Romans 6:23). I am overwhelmed by this incredible gift.

How is it that I can take this matter so seriously one moment and then barely think about it for days at a time? If not for God's mercy, you and I would have no hope. But the mercy of God overcame His perfect judgment of all sin when He sent us His Son Jesus. And so my soul and spirit rejoice with inexpressible joy, overwhelmed by His peace–His perfect, gentle, beautiful peace that cannot be explained.

> Grace and peace be multiplied to you through the knowledge of God and of Jesus our Lord. (2 Peter 1:2 MEV)

It's curious that just focusing my thoughts on Him and rejoicing in His precious gift of Christ escorts me into His presence, and I sense His immense joy when I have drawn near and responded to His quiet hello. I have chosen to stop and say hello back. I have made the conscious choice to once again pause and ask Him, "What are you thinking about, Lord? Am I in alignment with You?" I have chosen to listen to what is on His heart. I heard in my spirit, "I am thinking about you, Beloved. I have missed you, and I am delighted that you have drawn near to Me. I have so much to say. My love is powerful, eternal, perfect, and gentle—everything you need."

My eyes filled with tears of gratitude as I basked in the sweetness of the moment. Time stood still for me. My soul found the rest it had been craving. In the quiet of my heart, I then asked Him, "Lord, where on this imaginary scale do You say I am in knowing You?"

"Two."

I was suddenly embarrassed at my pride, aware that I knew so little of our awesome, Holy God, overwhelmed with understanding He wants us all to know Him so much more than we do.

I hope that you occasionally ask yourself the question, "How well do I know God today?" And when you do, I trust that you will ponder the truth that you can know Him more than you do, in ways you never thought possible. His immense love awaits you, like a beautiful river of refreshing water. No longer stay on the edge of His ocean of mercy and grace, but venture out past the shallow area into the depths of His love where you are surrounded and immersed in the treasures of His great goodness and astounding power.

How Well Do We Know God?

And we know that the Son of God has come, and he has given us understanding so that we can know the true God. And now we live in fellowship with the true God because we live in fellowship with his Son, Jesus Christ. He is the only true God, and he is eternal life. (1 John 5:20 NLT)

Reflections

Chapter 11
GOD'S JOYOUS LOVE FOR US

> The Lord is my shepherd, I lack nothing. He makes me lie down in green pastures, he leads me beside quiet waters, he refreshes my soul. He guides me along the right paths for his name's sake. (Psalm 23:1-3)

One Thursday night, a few of my sisters in Christ and I were visiting, praying, and worshiping God together. We were so overwhelmed by how good God is and were telling each other stories of His faithfulness to us. It was a beautiful evening after a rather tough week for me at work. I had almost chosen not to go meet with them because I was tired. But within me I sensed it was important to go, to be refreshed, and to focus on God instead of focusing on how weary I felt.

The next morning, as I read my Bible before getting ready for work, I sensed the Lord urging me to write. I immediately picked up my pen and journal and waited. I prayed as I settled my mind down and asked for the grace to hear only His sweet voice. A song arose within me:

> Show me, Lord, the beauty of Your face.
> Show me, Lord,
> The wonders of Your grace.
> Your awesomeness and power,
> The wisdom of Your Word,
> Show me, Lord, help me see
> Your kingdom come on earth.
>
> Help me, Lord, God of all,
> Grant me grace to see,
> All You've done, all You are,
> Increase the faith in me.
> Clean my heart and mind, Lord,
> I want to serve You well.
> Open my eyes, Jesus,
> To see Your kingdom grow.
>
> Lead me, Lord, God of all,
> Savior of the world,
> Use me, Lord, help me speak
> The power of Your Word.
> Lead me by Your Spirit,
> Your presence is my joy!
> Show me, Lord, help me, Lord,
> Lover of my soul!

God's Joyous Love For Us

He then surprised me by His exuberance as I found myself writing the following words. As I reflected upon the outpouring of His joy and love, I became aware that our worship the prior night had brought our Lord such delight that He naturally just wanted us to bask in the glory of His love.

> Rejoice in My presence, Beloved! Such joy and delights are here! My songs for you are to bless you and overwhelm you with My love. Do not restrict My Spirit because you think you are unworthy. Remember, because you have chosen Jesus My Son as your Redeemer and King, you are therefore worthy to receive from Me the abundance of all I Am. Consider the bounty of this truth!

> Rejoice! Sing and dance with joy and abandon as you fully receive My great love for you. Like a waterfall in the spring gushing forth tons of water per second, pouring down from the heights, so is My love for My people who know Me and love Me. Receive the abundance of it! Let the roar of it drown out the chatter and chaos and distractions of the world.

Then, as you sit by the still waters gathered together, rest. Come to Me and rest. Sit with Me and talk with Me. I desire that you desire intimacy of soul with Me, communion in the spirit.

Tell My people how immense and personal My love is.

Draw near.

Reflections

Chapter 12
WHEN WE WHISPER HIS NAME

> The Sovereign Lord will wipe away the tears from all faces. (Isaiah 25:8a)

Like you, a lot of things hinder my time with God. I keep meaning to settle down and read, journal or pray, but I am often easily distracted. One particular day my heart was heavy because of struggles my loved ones were burdened with. I finally stopped doing the dishes and checking for texts. I needed to be still.

I whispered, "Jesus, please help." What ended up on the page before me greatly encouraged me. I hurried to send it to my friend, who was in a season of great despair. I knew it was for her. Years later, it still encourages me as well...

> Beautiful is faith to me, Beloved. Even small whispers of faith from trembling lips bring Me honor and praise. Do not

despise days and seasons of trembling when walking with Me seems so hard, for I am carrying you. Believe Me when I tell you My great, fathomless love for you will never be extinguished, nor will it fade. My love for My own is eternal and perfect. I am holy.

Now little one, lift your eyes to heaven and speak My name. With joy I listen to your words of faith, and I bless every small act of obedience. When you speak My name, you declare I live, and this honors Me.

Your tears are not overlooked. I capture each one with tenderness as I hold you close to My merciful heart. It is true that in seasons like this you cannot sense My presence or hear My voice due to the spirit of discouragement overshadowing you, but do not be dismayed. I am closer than the air you breathe, for I dwell within your most secret being. Your spirit is eternally entwined with Mine. I know your every thought before you think it, and I love you, regardless of whether your thoughts are against Me or for Me.

I love you, My child. Just as you love your children regardless of the season of maturity they are in, even when they act foolishly or out of ignorance, you love them, do you not? Yes. And when they are struggling, weary, and fearful, you draw near to cover and comfort them with your prayers and your acts of love. Even when they do not recognize your acts of love, this does not make you love them less. No, you remember when you held them in your arms as babes and when you laughed together and sat quietly together doing simple things. You know they will turn to you again, so you wait patiently.

If you know how to do this with your children, is it not because this is how I am with My beloved children? Yes. And My love is superior to your love for your own. My love is unconditional. I love you. Believe.

When We Whisper His Name

I have loved you with an everlasting love; I have drawn you with unfailing kindness. (Jeremiah 31:3)

Reflections

Chapter 13
GOD DOES NOT CHANGE

> Every good and perfect gift is from above, coming down from the Father of the heavenly lights, who does not change like shifting shadows. (James 1:17)

For many years early in my Christian walk, I went to church on most Sundays, read the Bible off and on, and prayed as best as I knew how. When I became hungry to know God, one of the things I became increasingly aware of was that I didn't love God or other people like I knew I should. My busy life, selfish ways, and old habits kept me staying at a distance from Him.

As I read books about other Christians' experiences with God and heard other people talk about their walk with God, I was left perplexed as to why there was such a disconnect in my own faith walk and why some believers were able to have more intimacy of soul with God than others. I am so grateful that whenever I bring the cries of my heart to God that He answers my questions when I am ready to hear.

I am the Lord, and I do not change. My laws from days of old are still My laws today for this generation. This is truth.

Therefore, I require My church, My people, to seek Me and serve Me. Is not the greatest commandment to love and serve the Lord God and Him alone? My people serve many false gods, including their own plans and agendas. Why do so many not care about My plans? I am on the backburner of the lives of most people. They may think about Me on Sunday, but what about the other six days? Do they seek My opinion about their everyday plans and decisions? No, most do not. They may cry out to Me when perilous times come on them. They sometimes get mad at Me when their plans fail, although I did not instruct them to do that thing. I am only obligated to bless that which I instruct My own to do.

My people do not believe I love them and will care for them. If they did trust Me, they would not worry as they do. If they did believe Me, they would obey Me, My laws, and My ways.

Consider the law of love. Does not My Word say to love the Lord God with all your heart, mind, and strength? But most of My people do not love Me like this. They try to serve Me in their own ways. Most do not consider whether they love Me or not. This wounds My merciful heart because I long for fellowship with My people and to be their first love.

Also consider that My Word says to love one another as you love yourself. Do My people demonstrate such love for one another? Do they seek unity within the body of Christ corporately? Or, do they want to be entertained, served, and get their own way? My Word says that the world will know they are Christians by their love for one another. Sadly, this is not the reputation My people have in most communities. Is this your reputation?

Seek first My kingdom and My righteousness, and I will direct your path. Seek to know Me and love Me. Seek to know the holy Scriptures so that you will know the truth—the truth will set My people free. If you love Me, you will obey Me and My commands. If you do not know

My ways, then how will you obey Me? I desire all people to know My ways.

Be holy, for I am holy. Do you know what holiness is? Learn holiness. Search the Scriptures for the requirements of serving Me.

Just because Jesus saved your soul from eternal darkness, does not mean you can live as you like without consequence. All man does and says will someday be judged by the Holy One of God. Repent, therefore, of your ignorance of My Word, My ways, and My laws.

Seek Me while I may be found. Now is the time of My greatest mercy. Do not wait until it is convenient for you to serve Me, know Me and love Me, for the time of My return draws near. The time is short. Repent of your rebellion and pride. Run to My arms of grace and fall in love with Me. I am the lover of your soul.

God Does Not Change

In your unfailing love preserve my life, that I may obey the statutes of your mouth. Your word, Lord, is eternal; it stands firm in the heavens. (Psalm 119:88-89)

Reflections

Chapter 14
THE POWER OF GOD

> Let us then approach God's throne of grace with confidence, so that we may receive mercy and find grace to help us in our time of need. (Hebrews 4:16)

In response to my heart's yearning to know God more, I try to make it a point to read or listen to some Scriptures every day and intentionally think about His ways. Although many times I fail, He knows my motives and intentions, and I am grateful He continually draws me to Himself.

Many times in my commute to and from work I talk to God and tell Him all that is on my heart. As things in this world seem to get more and more out of control, at times it is easy to focus only on what I hear on the news. Like you, I can worry and get overwhelmed or fearful. But God always wants us to be grounded in the truth that He loves us, is in control, and is powerful to save us.

GOD STILL SPEAKS

One day when I was talking to God about the distressful things going on in the world, these words flowed from the pen in my hand:

> I, the Lord God Almighty, have given you a spirit of power and not of fear. The enemy lies to you and constantly waits to deceive you when there is an opportunity. Give him no opportunity. Fill your mind and heart with My Word of truth. Fight him with My Word; the authority you have in Christ is your power.
>
> Do not be overwhelmed with the calamities that go on around you. Stand on the Rock—Jesus Christ—your firm foundation. He lifts up those who humble themselves before My throne of holiness. There is no other god but Me. They all shall know that I Am the Lord. Hide yourself in Christ and pray for protection from pride.
>
> Christ stands at the door of your heart and knocks. Open your heart wide and come to the Lord, all you people! He longs for His Beloved—His church, His people—but many do not know His voice. The Spirit of God is deeply grieved

because so many of the people of the Most High do not believe His Word.

Humble yourself before My throne of power and holiness. Bow low, therefore, and know that I Am the Lord God. I am He who gives life and takes it back again. I desire all souls to be Mine, but they must submit to Me, they must believe Me, and they must hear My words of truth.

So few speak of My glory and power. My people are overwhelmed and preoccupied with the calamities in their lives. They do not worship Me in all things. They seek their own way and to explain it in their own words. But I desire they seek Me in the midst of the storms of their lives. My name is I AM. My Son Jesus is the Prince of Peace.

My words are life and are full of hope for My own, for those who receive Me. Open your hearts wide to Me. Hear My voice. I have so much more for you than you could ever comprehend. Ask for more of Me! I give abundantly to those who ask. I love you, My people.

He who forms the mountains, who creates the wind, and who reveals His thoughts to mankind, who turns dawn to darkness, and treads the heights of the earth—the Lord God Almighty is His name. (Amos 4:13)

Reflections

Chapter 15
HUMILITY OF SOUL

> Humble yourselves before the Lord, and
> he will lift you up. (James 4:10)

When The Lord first started mentioning humility of soul during my prayer time, I really wanted to grasp what it meant. What did it look like? How could I begin to live before God in such a way, to humble myself fully before Him, with all my emotions, personality, and humanity?

As I regularly do, I asked God to grant me understanding and to teach me. I researched the meaning of soul and humility. After many weeks of praying for insight on this matter, one day, with joy I sensed the Lord urge me to write.

> Humility of soul draws you to My Word and to My throne room of grace. It is pride that causes you to stumble and wobble in your faith. Pride says you should know what I will do and how I will

do it. Pride says that you should know My timing. Pride even causes you to worry, thinking you should be able to figure out the answers on your own and what to do when trying to protect yourself. Pride causes you to be offended by My ways.

Little one, don't you yet grasp that I know all things? Come to Me for the answers and direction you need, and be patient as I move in your life, for I reveal truth and wisdom as you are able to receive it. This is why you must pray for mercy and for greater faith, for protection from pride, for it is pride that causes mankind to reject My Word, My direction, and My plan. Pride is the chief sin.

My ways are not your ways. My ways are not the ways of mankind, so they will not usually make sense to you. Seek the truths of the Scriptures, and you will see that this has always been My way. I do the miraculous and the foolish to confound the wise and show them their wisdom is nothing apart from My grace, favor, and mercy.

Humility of soul occurs when you lay down your entire self at the cross of Christ and come to Me empty-handed with only your faith in My love for you, trusting Me with everything, depending on Me for everything, relying on My promises proclaimed in My Word.

Therefore, Beloved, always bring all your emotions and your entire being to My alter and allow Me to help you navigate your way to holiness.

Then he (the angel) said, "Don't be afraid, Daniel. Since the first day you began to pray for understanding and to humble yourself before your God, your request has been heard in heaven. I have come in answer to your prayer. (Daniel 10:12 NLT)

Reflections

Chapter 16
THE VALUE OF STRUGGLES

> I will refresh the weary and satisfy the faint. (Jeremiah 31:25)

2010 was a long, arduous year for me. I was grieving the recent deaths of my father, a dear friend's mother, and another precious friend's brother. I was up to my eyeballs in paperwork administering my parents' trust. Also, my husband Don and I were entangled in a multiyear law suit because we had to close our business; it was the death of our dream. Financially, things were extremely difficult due to the costs of the litigation. We both were mentally exhausted and overwhelmed–the stress of it all was negatively affecting our health. Many of our friends and loved ones were also struggling financially, and a few were losing their homes due to the aftermath of the economic downturn. It was just a very rough time.

In the midst of all the turmoil, God was so very faithful to provide for us, often in surprising and creative ways. Money being so tight was frustrating and stressful, but

The Value Of Struggles

by God's grace we lacked nothing. I was more aware of those who were homeless, those who struggled so much more than I. Somehow we were able to pay our bills, and by God's mercy, the intense struggles brought Don and me even closer together than we had been previously. We held on to each other and the hope that God would bring us through.

That summer it was hard for me to settle down and pray, read my Bible, or write in my journal. I was numb, just struggling with the harshness of life, and desperate for God to bring us through that grueling desert season. God had been continually reminding me that He would not forsake us, that He loved us, and that He had a good plan for our lives. We could not see it though. We often just wanted to run away and hide.

After the trial ended, we anxiously waited for nearly two months to hear the final ruling from the court. A note from my journal that September reveals my heart:

> I feel so stuck, so constrained. Too many distractions, so much waiting. God is teaching me to truly trust Him, teaching me to wait on His timing. I sense He wants me to get to the point where I desire Him more than anything else—He reminds me that *He* is the gift. Do I truly believe God concerning all He has promised?

A week later as I was weeping before God, crying out for yet another miracle, He so gently calmed me down. I opened my journal and began writing the words pouring into my mind:

> I who have hidden you in the cleft of the rock, it is I who speak to you. Listen closely; do not turn away. Do not doubt. Believe Me, for I am trustworthy and true.
>
> Be at peace. My peace I give you. It is a perfect covering. Here in My sanctuary your spirit hears the truth and is comforted. In the solitude you find rest for your soul and focus your thoughts on Me. In the quiet you can hear My voice as I soothe your many anxieties. I alone am worthy of your praise.
>
> Recall all of My acts of faithfulness to you, little one. Do not forget the joys of knowing intimacy of soul with Me. There are no words for such delights as being in My presence and surrounded by My glory. Childlike faith delights Me. When you worry, you have taken your eyes off of Me and set your mind on your own perspective instead of Mine. My child, look to Me again; see Me smile at you.

The Value Of Struggles

> Your struggle is not hidden from My eyes, and I look diligently for your acts of faith and words of trust, and I remember them. Your songs of joy thrill My spirit, and angels join in to worship Me. My ministering spirits are sent to you when tears well in your eyes. Never doubt this.

The court ultimately ruled in our favor. It was an exhausting, humbling and intense season in which God proved Himself faithful to protect and carry us. During that difficult year, the Lord also gave me this little poem that still encourages me:

> Beautiful faith is blooming:
> roots grow deep in Christ.
> Honor and glory will follow
> for those who believe My words of life.
>
> Struggles are meant to strengthen,
> tears wash clean the soul,
> prayers lift up your face towards Me,
> the Living One, God of all.
>
> Even in winter when trees look dead,
> we know their life is hidden,
> and you, Beloved, are like that tree,
> Your life is hidden in Me.

GOD STILL SPEAKS

The sun brings light and warmth to you,
and springtime always comes;
it is welcomed by all creation,
and life bursts forth again.

No one but God of creation
knows the winter growth,
and sees the struggles of a soul
as winter storms push to and fro.

But God is faithful, His promises true,
enduring every season;
winter is needed as much as spring,
summer, and autumn—
each have a reason.

Each brings forth a time of growth,
Some harsh, some joyous and sweet;
Despise not the seasons of life and faith,
I work all together for My glory.

Reflections

Chapter 17
GOD IN THE LITTLE THINGS

> I will consider all your works and meditate on all your mighty deeds. (Psalm 77:12)

There is a large green belt of open land that stretches out for miles along the Pacific coast near my home. The green belt ends abruptly at a bluff, which drops about sixty feet down to the beach. It is a beautiful and peaceful escape from the craziness of daily life, and I always enjoy taking our dog Tasha for walks there.

I often talk to God about all that is on my heart during these walks and allow Tasha to run free in the open field. Sometimes I am very aware of the Lord answering a question that has been on my heart or just causing me to understand something I previously did not grasp. It is often humorous and always precious to me when the Lord shows me striking similarities between how

I care for Tasha and watch out for her best interests, and how He cares for and protects me.

One winter day in 2010, not too long after my father had passed away, and before the litigation was complete, I poured out my heart in my journal:

It is stormy outside, and here in my soul it also is storming. I fight against myself it seems. I want to sit with God and pray, to listen and learn. Yet I am so restless inside, so easily distracted by very insignificant things.

Lord God, I am overwhelmed by Your immense love, grace, and patience with me. I praise You for Your mercy. The enemy is relentless in his onslaught of distractions, like a machine gun, rapidly firing thoughts of "do this, do that, do just one more thing!" And in the midst of it all I hear Your voice, Lord, whispering to me to come and sit with You, to rest my mind and soak in Your Word.

Please wrap Your protective arms around me, my Jesus. Put Your hands over the ears of my mind and soul so that I can only hear Your sweet voice. I am weary at the intensity of the battle, the length of it, the extent of it. When will You grant me a season of rest? Oh, I long for a day of quiet in my soul, a day of just Your presence and peace in my mind. Lord, You know how much I love You and how I long to be faithful to You. Grant me the grace to please You today by honoring You with my thoughts and my time. Put songs of joy in my heart and words of praise on my tongue.

Grant me focus, Lord. Do not let me forget what You taught me yesterday as I walked Tasha. We went down onto the beach, and she ran way ahead of me to chase the birds. I went the same direction south that I normally do, but took a higher path along the bluff edge, a different path. Suddenly, Tasha realized she could not see me from where she was playing near the water's edge. She ran to find me, taking the usual path to the bluff top where she was with me last. I saw her run up from the beach to the top of the bluff, disappearing from my view. Concerned where she would head off to, I quickly ran back up the path to the bluff top to find her searching for me. "Here I am, Tasha," I called out. She ran back to me, both of us relieved to be united again.

Lord, You showed me that I must keep my eyes on You, for You often lead me in a new way. If I am too busy, distracted, or restless, I can easily lose sight of You and go back to where I was with You last. You then pursue me as You know I am searching for You. Thank You for leading me on a new, higher path. Keep me close to You. Keep my eyes on You so that I won't be backtracking so often. I want to be fully prepared for what You have next for me. I want to be readily obedient to You, expectant that You are leading me for the good of Your kingdom. Thank you for using the little things in my daily life to teach me wonderful truths about Your profound love.

> I am the Lord your God, who teaches you what is best for you, who directs you in the way you should go. (Isaiah 48:7)

REFLECTIONS

Chapter 18
THE PEACE OF GOD

> Do not be anxious about anything, but in every situation, by prayer and petition, with thanksgiving, present your requests to God. And the peace of God, which transcends all understanding, will guard your hearts and your minds in Christ Jesus. (Philippians 4:6-7)

The world in which we live is increasingly stressful and dangerous. I am sure you are no different than I in that the heaviness of life often causes you to worry and be afraid. During one particularly burdensome season, I again found myself worrying more and praying less. Soon, I was so focused on the problems that I struggled to think about anything else.

I was reminded that God's peace is His signature on my soul and mind, evidence of my time spent with Him and in His Word. I must deliberately choose to spend time with Jesus and pour out my concerns before Him. He has shown me time and time again that even in difficult times, His peace surpasses understanding and is meant to sustain and strengthen us. He desires our faith to be childlike, relevant, and transparent. He wants to shine His light and love through our lives to the hurting world around us. Worry inhibits our ability to do this.

He wants our words and actions to reflect the peace and power of Christ in our lives, but sadly, most of us do not live such lives consistently as He desires. I am painfully aware of my stumbling, and when I take my eyes off Him and remove His power from the equation, my peace evaporates. This keeps me humble before Him, longing to be more consistent in my faith walk with Him.

I poured my coffee and sat down to enjoy it as I was trying to wake up one foggy morning. As is sometimes the case, the only prayer I could muster that day was a whispered, "Help me, Jesus, I am overwhelmed." He then encouraged me with these words:

> I am the God of peace. I do not cause you to be anxious, restless, and worried; that comes from the enemy, who desires that you not live in My rest and peace. Then the enemy can cause you to focus on anything else but Me. Danger exists for you when you take your eyes off of

me, for in Christ alone are you safe from destruction and pride. Pride causes you to be consumed with trying to figure things out on your own. Trust asks, "What do you want me to do, Lord?"

Be at peace and rest in Me. Cast down and reject those anxious thoughts and worries that take your eyes off of Me, the risen One. I alone can give clear direction. The enemy seeks to confuse and mislead you. However, in Christ you are secure and surefooted, not wavering or wandering. I give you My confidence while the enemy causes you to feel insecure, fearful, and cowering in your own weakness.

Be of good cheer, dear one: I have overcome the enemy! Bring each thought to Me. I am Jesus Christ, son of the Living God who is glorified forever.

Today is a new day to seek the Lord God Almighty, to search for Him and find Him, to draw near to Him in His Word and in prayer. Seek the Lord in all things—every decision, every choice. Seek His direction. He will direct you as you wait on

Him. This is truth, and this is how you are to walk uprightly before the Living God. This is how you honor Him and bring Him delight: by obedience to His Word and to the leading of His Spirit.

Holiness requires obedience, submission, and a humble heart that loves mercy. This honors God and causes the heavens to open up and pour blessings into your life.

Consider these words, My child. Be at peace and rest in Me.

REFLECTIONS

Chapter 19
FORGIVENESS AND GROWING IN FAITH

> This righteousness is given through faith in Jesus Christ to all who believe. (Romans 3:22)

I have observed that some who know the Bible do not seem to understand the ways of God's heart because their knowledge is head knowledge and not knowledge derived from a spiritual life in communion with God. For those who do not know the Bible well, their knowledge of God is extremely limited, and they are vulnerable to fall for the many lies of the enemy and the world. I was like that early in my Christian walk.

Thankfully, I was told about Bible Study Fellowship (BSF) in 1989 and I ventured into a powerful, five-year structured study of God's Word. This gave me a good biblical foundation to grow in my faith. One key takeaway from this chapter of my life is that we each must make a conscious effort to continue to grow in our faith and understanding of God's Word and His ways. To be intentional with our God-time is critical.

I became very involved with California Women's Retreat (CWR), an outstanding organization focused on bringing Christ-centered, biblically-based speakers and musicians to women needing soul-rest and encouragement in their faith. Over the last thirty years, I have had the privilege of working alongside dozens of precious CWR women who love Jesus, and many have become life-long friends. The prayers, discipleship, and love these have poured into my life have been integral to my emotional healing and spiritual growth. It is God's way that we grow in our faith alongside other believers.

> Let us not neglect our meeting together, as some people do, but encourage one another, especially now that the day of his return is drawing near. (Hebrews 10:25)

God is also continually teaching me about the expansiveness of life in Christ. I have learned that I am to ask myself questions about my spiritual health and to ask Jesus what His perspective is. Am I growing in my faith, or am I stagnant? Do I hunger for more of God's presence? When was the last time I diligently searched the Scriptures for answers to my hardest questions and to sooth my anxious mind? Am I desperate for a move of God in my life?

I recall a significant event in my spiritual journey which occurred after church one Sunday in August 2004. I sat in my car contemplating the pastor's message about our need to forgive others. He said that when God causes us to look back on our life it is never to shame us or re-open wounds, but to heal us. As I sat there watching everyone else drive away, the Lord showed me I was not as happy as I thought I was, that I needed healing in my heart. I asked God to open my mind and show me what I needed healing of. And He did.

First, I became aware there was anger in my heart buried so deep by pain that I was blind to its existence. He showed me that this was what brought heaviness to my spirit off and on, but I didn't know why. I was perplexed to realize there could be such pain and anger which I had not dealt with. I vividly recall that as I searched my soul God gently revealed to me each event, each person who wounded me, from my childhood years to the present. As I acknowledged each painful interaction, I laid down each one at the foot of the cross asking Christ to cover me and heal me of my pain and anger. He allowed me to think about each situation only long enough for me to realize the truth and to give it to Him.

Forgiveness And Growing In Faith

Once brought into the light of His love, Jesus helped me forgive each person, one by one. This included forgiving myself for some foolish choices I had made which forever changed the course of my life. This healing time continued for over an hour. The freedom and release which I experienced that day was beautiful, refreshing and brought peace to my soul which I had not known before. I was able to grasp in a new way, the grace of God to heal as I trusted Him with my whole heart.

Forgiving removed previously unseen blockages in my ability to grow in my faith. Forgiving did not condone the hurtful behavior others inflicted on me – it set my spirit free to be at peace and release the burden to God.

Although it can be a struggle to lay aside all the distractions of this life for just a little while, it is always beneficial to make time to quiet myself in His presence. Today I again found myself praying, "Lord, please search my heart and mind. Expose all of the junk that is getting in the way of the life of power and unity with Christ that You desire for me."

Perhaps today you, too, might take the time to ask God to reveal yourself to you. Whom do you need to forgive? Whom do you need to reach out to? How is pride polluting your spiritual walk? What idols need to be torn down? These are just some of the questions I occasionally ask myself. It is a lifelong journey to mature in our faith. I am grateful that He uses every step of every season in this incredible journey, never wasting anything.

I pray that God would heal the broken places in your soul that keep you from fully knowing His astounding love, power, and wisdom. If you let Him, over time He will set you free from the chains of worry, doubt, fear, offense, and hurt which keep you from thriving and living the amazing life of power and love made possible by Christ's death and resurrection. This is the joy He desires for you: that you would know He is the Lord God of all and will grasp His immense love for you, that you would know *you* are His beloved.

> Beloved of the Lord, hear My call. Stand firm on My promises and on all My words, for they are faithful and true. I alone am the faithful One. I am He who loves the lost. I died for all souls, and I love My own tenderly and fiercely. I vigorously defend the honor of My name, so ask the Father in My name, Jesus, and give My Father in heaven all the glory!
>
> Seek My will in all you think and do. Listen intently to My words of truth and

search the holy Scriptures with diligence to uncover the treasures of the mysteries of My kingdom. This is your power and security, Beloved: that you know My Word, love My Word, and believe My Word. Rely on nothing else. This is your firm foundation; I am the rock on which you stand with My authority and power.

Forgive freely. Be wise and gentle. Speak truth. I am He who sees all. Every thought and motive of every soul is laid bare before Me. No one is innocent before Me, and only those who hide themselves in Christ's righteousness are shown mercy and forgiven of all sins against Father God. Contemplate these words, Beloved.

Make allowance for each other's faults, and forgive anyone who offends you. Remember, the Lord forgave you, so you must forgive others. (Colossians 3:13 NLT)

Reflections

Chapter 20
THE REST OF GOD

> Therefore, since the promise of entering his rest still stands, let us be careful that none of you be found to have fallen short of it. (Hebrews 4:1)

God has for us the gift of rest that only He can provide to our minds and souls. Sabbath rest is spoken of quite often in the Bible. The Sabbath is a day of rest from our work. Just as God created the world in six days and rested on the seventh, He desires that we rest from our six days of weekly labor and take one day a week to focus on Him and enjoy His blessings. I am not very good at taking a day to rest, yet it is a goal I strive for. It seems there is always too much to do. However, I didn't know about the rest of being in God's presence until He taught me. I am still learning and will continue this learning process as long as I live, but I choose to learn.

One day as I was trying to settle down and rest my mind and soul, I sat with my Bible and journal, asking

God to help me. I was inspired to write the following on the empty page before me:

> Beloved, learn of Me. Sit here with Me and rest. Do nothing but rest. Do nothing but trust Me to do everything. This is My rest in Christ Jesus for you, given freely, yet you must obey, listen, and do it—that is, rest. Here you will find the riches of My graces and mercies in Christ Jesus. Here in the storehouse of My abundance is the rest you require.
>
> Why do you strive so? You desire to please Me, and this delights Me. But truly, to please Me is to receive all I have done for you, all I have freely given to you. Desire to grasp and receive My great love for you. I will show you how; I will teach you.
>
> Close your eyes and learn to see in the spirit. Listen with your spiritual ears. Hear what My Spirit says to you: "Beloved, come to Me, you who are weary and heavy burdened, and I will give you rest. You just need to come to Me, and I will do the rest."

The Rest Of God

Because you love Jesus, My precious and eternal Son, great graces are yours, Beloved. Seek My words of truth, and My Spirit will instruct you. To be sitting with Christ and in Christ requires you to rest. Struggle not against Me. Just rest in Me. See and embrace the riches of My goodness.

Consider these words, My child.

Then Jesus said, "Let's go off by ourselves to a quiet place and rest awhile." (Mark 6:31 NLT)

Reflections

Chapter 21
MONITORING MY THOUGHT LIFE

> Do not conform to the pattern of this world, but be transformed by the renewing of your mind. Then you will be able to test and approve what God's will is—his good, pleasing and perfect will. (Romans 12:2)

It was 2012 and after an unusually stressful year at work, my job was eliminated, and I found myself unemployed. I was in great need of soul rest. Thankfully, I was given a severance package that allowed me to take a few months off and figure out who I was apart from my day job. Like many people, I have a tendency to throw myself into my work, and in the process, I sometimes lose myself in it, which is not a good thing. Doing so often results in no margin in my life for quality time with Jesus, my husband, my loved ones, or myself to mentally and emotionally process what is happening in my life.

I so greatly enjoyed those months off. I was eating healthier, spending long weekends with Don visiting our favorite places, walking almost every day with my dog Tasha out on the bluff, and spending lots of time with a dear friend who was chronically ill. I was even able to finish reading some books that I had started more than once. Much to my dismay, I never did get the workroom decluttered. However, I got in the habit of watching a lot of TV and found my mind getting lazy. Thankfully, after a while, my soul found balance again, and I started writing in my journal regularly, delighting in my relationship with God. I wrote this poem that summer:

> How long will I be foolish?
> So headstrong yet so weak,
> I hear His voice and hear His call,
> yet still I wait; why don't I seek?
>
> I know His love, I need His all,
> yet pride gets in the way,
> I choose the foolish things to do
> instead of doing what He says.
>
> I hear the words inside my head,
> "Give in to Me, Beloved."
> My heart, it softens as I yield.
> I turn and receive comfort.

Monitoring My Thought Life

Lord God, Your love astounds me.
Lord God, Your mercy shines.
A tune plays gently in my mind:
*"Lean into Me, dear child,
remember you are Mine."*

I turn my eyes to seek You;
I turn my mind to truth.
Steadfastly You gaze at me,
Your love—it pulls me through.

I was enjoying the season of rest but began getting annoyed at myself that so much time was just slipping by. I would look back on a week and wonder to myself, *What did I accomplish? How is it possible I didn't get anything at all done on my to-do list?* I recall numerous times watching TV for the entire day, and by evening I was saddened at the realization I had seemed to have wasted a day of my life, a day which could never be lived again; there are no do-overs. I wish I could say this happens less frequently than it actually does.

A few weeks later, as I was enjoying time with the Lord, the following flowed out of my pen:

> Today is a new day to serve Me, little one. Be strong in Christ your Savior. The Holy Spirit of God is your witness to testify before Me of the motives and intentions

of your heart. Every heart cry, every yearning in your spirit, I hear, I see, I know.

I am well pleased with your tender heart toward Me, but I am grieved at your ease of allowing your mind to wander aimlessly. You allow the enemy to lead your mind to a wasteland of empty thoughts, which leaves you weak and confused. It should not be so.

My Spirit is a spirit of love, power, and a sound mind—a disciplined mind. This requires you to exercise self-control, controlling where your thoughts wander off to. Be continually aware that the enemy wants you to be powerless and ineffective for My kingdom work. Therefore, turn your thoughts to Me, to My Word, and pray. Learn to do this continually. Like feeding your body, you must feed your mind and spirit.

Nourish yourself by resting in My presence. This rest is worship, reading My Word, contemplating My words, seeking increased understanding, and drawing ever closer to Me, the Lord of all.

MONITORING MY THOUGHT LIFE

Soak in My power, joy, and peace. Avail yourself to Me at all times. Be ever seeking to draw closer to Me. This starts in your heart and mind. Be deliberate in what you think about. Focus intentionally on My promises and listen intently to My Spirit. My written Word confirms what My Spirit tells you.

Believe I am strong enough to protect you from all the attacks of the enemy. The mind of Christ is your head armor—yes, the helmet of salvation. Bring every thought captive to Christ Jesus. Lay lazy thoughts at His cross. An empty mind is what the enemy wants, but I grant you a full and alert mind in alignment with My thoughts.

My power is in My Word. Put My Word in your mouth. Write My words on the tablets of your mind. Replace wandering, lazy thoughts with conversations with Me, your God and Savior. It is good to talk to Me aloud when you can; it is always good to sing My praises. It is excellent to walk with Me and to allow Me to lead you. I am Jesus; I am the Good Shepherd. Listen for My voice.

You will keep in perfect peace all who trust in you, all whose thoughts are fixed on you! (Isaiah 26:3 NLT)

Reflections

Chapter 22
WHEN FAITH IS WEARY

> As for you, O Lord, you will not restrain your mercy from me, your steadfast love and your faithfulness will ever preserve me! For evils have encompassed me beyond number; my failures have overtaken me, and I cannot see; they are more than the hairs on my head; my heart fails me. Be pleased to deliver me! O Lord, make haste to help me! (Psalm 40:11–13)

When King David wrote Psalm 40, this song to his God, his faith was weary. David knew God would be faithful to care for him based on his prior experiences with Him, so throughout the song, David encourages his own soul with words of faith. As is often the case with me, his praise to God is interwoven with cries for mercy and help. My prayers are often as simple as "I trust you Jesus, and I need you to help me today." There are times I can only cry out in desperation, "I need You to fix this, Lord. You are the only one who can!"

The Bible is full of promises that God will reward our tiny and large acts of faith, such as Proverbs 22:4, which says, "The reward for humility and fear of the Lord is riches and honor and life." When all is going well in my life, I can read that with a smile on my face and say to myself, "Yes, this is true. God is good." However, when things go sour and life is hard, it is easy for me to say to myself, "I guess the reward will be only seen on other side of eternity."

Why do we tend to focus so much on the hard stuff in seasons of difficulty and get so easily discouraged and fall into a faith crisis? This I have learned to be true: God wants us to be steadfast in faith during the storms of life as well as when all is going incredibly well.

So how do we encourage our soul when our faith is weary? I often look to the Psalms for help with this during times of difficulty, and when it is hard to pray. David was so great at being brutally honest with God about his situation, his fears, his failures, and the unwarranted attacks of his enemies. David was a valiant warrior, and yet interwoven with his heart cries are whispers of faith, remembering how God had been faithful in the past and telling anyone who would listen that God will continue to be faithful.

When I struggle to pray, I often read the Psalms to myself, sometimes reading them out loud to encourage my soul and to remind myself that God indeed is faithful, He owns time, and He loves me.

Beloved, it is true I own time. I am never in a hurry. I see the full scope of My eternal plan for your life, and it is very good. The enemy wants to crush your faith, but I will protect it as it is most precious to Me. Yes, life will be very hard at times for you live in a fallen world, and the attacks of the enemy are relentless to discourage souls. And I do allow many things you do not understand, but these situations are to be seen from the eternal perspective—My perspective.

My goal is to mature you in Christ and prepare you for eternity in My presence. The enemy wants you to think this life on Earth is all there is. Do not listen to his lies. The truth is exclaimed throughout the holy Scriptures that I am in the process of redeeming this fallen world.

Consider how it was when you remodeled your kitchen. First, all the old had to be taken away, and the house was a mess for a couple of months while the reconstruction was underway. It was hard to envision how nice it would look when the remodel would be done, but you trusted the process. Even when there were setbacks, you continued to keep your mind on the completed remodel. When it was done, you were well pleased. In fact, you still enjoy the results of that hard work.

So is the case with My process of reshaping, remodeling, and restoring this fallen world. While the reconstruction has been underway for a long time from man's perspective, you are to understand that from My perspective, the project is on track. My plans are not thwarted by the plans of evil men or the strategies of the enemies of My kingdom. From man's perspective, bad things happen to good people. However, is it not also true that good things happen to evil people? Yes.

My process of redemption does not make sense to mankind. This is where faith is crucial—faith in My project of the redemption of all of creation, faith in My ability to make all things work together for the good of My kingdom. On this side of eternity, it is sometimes extremely difficult to see that I am in control, but be assured: I Am. You may even be angry at Me for allowing evil in the world, but I ask you to trust Me, little one of faith.

When you pass from this earthly world to the eternal, you will see the full scope of My plan and worship Me for all eternity. This life of yours is like a breath, a wisp of smoke in comparison to eternity. However, your life is of such incredibly high value to Me that I sent My son Jesus to redeem your soul from the ravages of sin, from the eternal consequences of the fall of man. Jesus entered the world of mankind to show each person how great My love is for all the world.

So how does this relate to your current difficulty, your current weariness of soul and wobbling faith? Your salvation is dependent on one thing: believing what Jesus did for you on the cross. I do all the rest. This is grace. This is mercy. Yes, your part is to keep your eyes on Me and learn My ways revealed in My Word. These things make the journey more peaceful and secure for you. Many choose not to learn My ways, and their life is a darker path because of the confusion and lack of truth in their soul. You know it is true that it is in the difficult seasons that you draw the closest to Me. This is how it is meant to be, for the pride of man is the chief sin, the largest obstacle, in walking close with Me.

If all were to go perfectly well for you at all times, you would think you have no need of Me; you would even think it is all going well because of how clever and talented you are. You know this is true. It is when difficulties arise that even people who do not yet know Me will cry out to Me for help. Without even thinking, they say, "Oh, God!" This is how I draw souls to Myself to save them from the ravages of fallen humanity.

When Faith Is Weary

What about souls who have already committed themselves to My eternal care by accepting My gift of salvation and choosing to follow Jesus? Why then do they also have such struggles in this world and with their faith? Consider again the remodel project in your home. It is your home; you want it to be the best it can be, so you invest your money, time, and energy into improving it. You are My own because you accepted Jesus as your Savior. Therefore, My Spirit lives in you; you are My home.

It is not in your best interest for Me to leave you just as you are or just as you were when you first accepted My gift of love. No, I love you far too much to leave you as you are. I am continually in the process of refining your faith, restoring what was lost, transforming you into the likeness of My Son for My glory. Like a good workout, "no pain, no gain." You are right that this seems harsh, but your soul is far too valuable to Me to leave you in your uncompleted state of reconstruction.

Trust Me to bring you through even this faith crisis. I have shown Myself faithful to you by saving your soul when you were still My enemy, so indeed I will continue to show Myself faithful by continually recreating you to be the person I know you can be in Christ, the fullness of My glory.

Put on your new nature, and be renewed as you learn to know your Creator and become like him. (Colossians 3:10 NLT)

Reflections

Chapter 23
THE LIGHT OF GOD

Jesus said, "I am the light of the world. Whoever follows me will never walk in darkness, but will have the light of life." (John 8:12)

There are times when I am busy doing various tasks, and in the middle of it I find myself highly aware of God's nearness. If I am not in too much of a hurry to respond, I pause and typically find myself smiling, thanking Him, grateful that I noticed Him drawing me to Himself. This happened one stormy, winter day a few years ago. A single candle was burning on my kitchen table, adding a hint of cinnamon to the air. I chose to stop what I was doing, moved to sit and write down my thoughts:

> Beautiful light, pure light, holiness and power–these are Your garments, Lord God Almighty.

The Light Of God

Who are we that You love us so? We have done nothing to deserve Your immense love, mercy, and kindness. Even when we try to walk uprightly before You, we often fail because of our weakness, pride, unbelief, and fear. No one is innocent before You, Lord God. Yet You, in Your astounding mercy, cover those who love Your Son with the garment of His perfection so that we can come boldly into Your throne room of grace in our time of need to seek help and worship You. What joys there are in Your presence! Who can grasp it?

I am like this small candle before me, burning but a single flame. That flame is the light that You have put in me to bring hope and life to those in darkness of soul. Help me shine Your light. You, Lord God, are like the air surrounding me, vast and immeasurable. You are the fuel for my fire, and I belong to You, created for the sole purpose of loving You, serving You, knowing You, delighting in Your presence and Your Word.

Help me declare to all who will listen that the Lord lives, and He is the Lord

> God Almighty, Creator of all that is seen and unseen. You are the Lord of heaven's armies, the Savior of all people who call on the name of the Lord and trust Jesus as their Savior. You are King of kings and Lord of lords. Nothing is too hard for You, my God. Forgive me for the countless opportunities lost when I stayed silent about You. Please grant new opportunities for me to tell others how amazing You are!

I sat listening to the wind howling, rain pounding on the roof—what a contrast to the peace I felt. God's response then coursed through my writing hand:

> Dear one, there is nothing more beautiful, more precious, more valuable to Me than ones faith in Christ. To believe Me and My Word—this is faith. To love and serve Jesus the Christ, My Son, is to believe Me, love Me, and serve Me. Life is in My presence; joy is My gift to you, Beloved.
>
> My peace is the robe you are to wear; Christ's righteousness is your strength and honor. Wisdom comes forth from My mouth for your healing, instruction, and

strength. You are not to fear anything, and you are to obey My words of life.

Pray, Beloved. Pray for My bride, the church: for holiness and a heart fully devoted to Me. My return draws near, and My bride is not ready. You are right that there is much foolishness and deceit in the world, so My people must shine My light–a spotlight of truth, full of power to save that which is lost, to redeem the oppressed and those in bondage. My light is My Word of truth.

I am the light of the world, says the Lord! I am He who lives forever. I am He who gives life! Amen.

Reflections

Chapter 24
THE POWER OF REJECTING LIES AND EMBRACING GOD'S TRUTH

> Jesus said, "If you hold to my teaching, you are really my disciples. Then you will know the truth, and the truth will set you free." (John 8:31-32)

Words spoken by those we care for can go very deep into our soul. Loving words strengthen us and give us courage. But harsh words can wound our souls.

For many years I struggled with unkind words spoken to me which I knew were not true: harsh or mean words spoken in selfishness, jealousy, foolishness, anger or pain. My logical mind would tell me I should dismiss the lies. And if I dared share them with a trusted friend, they would remind me those things were not true. But for some unknown reason I would keep hold of some and believe them anyway. I am grateful that when I am ready to receive healing, Jesus gently opens my mind to the truth. Truth about who I am from His perspective. I then must choose to believe Him, or continue to believe the lies which keep me insecure and hurting inside.

> Beloved, love My Word. Embrace the truths revealed in the Bible; this is My gift to mankind. This revelation of Who I AM and how I relate to people in all the Earth has not changed, nor will it ever change. The truths of My great love for My creation cannot be underestimated. The power of it changes everything. It is intended to change each and every person when they hear and receive the truth about what Jesus did for them. It is intended to change them from rebelling against Me and My ways and cause them to run to My arms of grace for freedom and peace with Me.
>
> But people must continually saturate their minds with the truth of My Word to dispel the years of lies and twisted truths that have polluted their thinking. Some lies are deeply engrained in their minds due to pain and hardship and the rejection of man. But My truths bring healing,

grace and light to the darkness of a mind trapped in lies. It is each person's choice to receive Me or reject Me each day. This is true for Christians and unbelievers alike. Even one of My own can be led astray by lies if they are not very careful.

The enemy of your soul is skilled at subtly distorting My truth. Like water dripping from a faucet, the enemy drips little lies into your mind every day–lies about Me, who I am, and what I am able to do. If you do not reject the lies immediately, you end up contemplating them and listening to the evil whispers of the enemy who says, "God is not able to fix this situation," "God let you down," "Your faith is not strong enough to get you through this," "Your faith is in vain," and "Did you really hear from God about that?"

Notice the strategy of the enemy: to sway you to believe that I don't love you, that I don't speak to you, that My eternal gift is beyond your reach. Do not believe these lies.

Most people do not recognize a subtle twisting of the truth when they hear it because they do not reflect upon My holy Scriptures each day. My Word is living and powerful to shine light and hope into darkness and dispel despair.

Why do My own think that they can survive spiritually without taking spiritual nourishment daily? How long can a person live without water? A few days? I tell you the truth, Beloved: if a soul is not moving toward Me, then they are moving away from Me. My Word and My Spirit are meant to be your daily nourishment and to draw you to My merciful heart. It is a daily, moment-by-moment choice. I love you, Beloved. Believe Me.

I sat at my kitchen table contemplating all the Lord had just spoken to my heart, I re-read the words on the page in front of me a few times and thinking how easy it is to listen to 'old tapes' which can replay in my mind when I am discouraged – lies so easy to ponder. Pen in hand, my heart responded:

My Lord Jesus, help me to steadfastly keep my eyes on You. Change my heart so that I am singularly devoted to You and to Your Word of life. Change my heart that I would love Your Word more than the ways of the world. Protect me from the lies of the enemy and grant me spiritual discernment that I would detect lies and quickly reject them.

Cause me to turn to You and bring my thoughts to You about all matters so You can cleanse my heart and mind of all unrighteousness and purify me with Your great love. Open my mind to really grasp how much You love me. Help me hear Your love cry for your people as I read Your Word.

Protect my wounded heart as You heal me with Your Word. Each time I read the Scriptures, help me submit to Your Holy Spirit and ask You to open my mind to Your truth. Help me apply Your Word to my life each day with wisdom.

I am overwhelmed by Your great love for Your creation, Lord. I sense the grief in Your heart when Your beloved people are misled and reject You due to fear, being wounded, or their lack of knowing You and Your Word. I praise You that You continually pursue us, Lord!

Thank you for never giving up on us and for granting us Your Word, Your Son Jesus, Your Holy Spirit, and the fellowship of believers who love You and are seeking You. Help us love You more each day, and open our eyes to see Your great love for us today. You are the God of today!

For the word of God is alive and active. Sharper than any double-edged sword, it penetrates even to dividing soul and spirit, joints and marrow; it judges the thoughts and attitudes of the heart. (Hebrews 4:12)

Reflections

Chapter 25
THE BLESSING OF BELIEVING GOD

> Blessed are those who hunger and thirst for righteousness, for they will be filled. (Matthew 5:6)

It was very late, and I couldn't sleep. I sensed in my spirit I should get up and write. As I sat in the darkness of my living room, I heard in my spirit, "Enjoy My presence." His words surprised me. Such tender and amazing words—the God of all creation wants to commune with us!

And then I started thinking about work. Why do I do that? My mind then turned to my precious loved ones, and I brought their needs to God. "Lord, You are the only One who can change their situation. Help them." I whispered their names one by one. I sensed God's peace wrap around me. Such grace.

As often as I ignore Him because I am so focused on everything else going on in my life, I am amazed He still waits for me to turn my thoughts to Him, draw near, and rest in His presence. The fact that He enjoys spending time with me is surprising. I don't consider myself to be that interesting that Jesus would want to just be with me, but He does. Responding to His voice as He woos me and draws me near honors Him. He is my audience of One, and He equally wants to commune with you, too. Never doubt it.

"Lord, I deeply desire to be more aware of Your presence, to be able to tune my thoughts and ears to You more each day. Sometimes I hear You so clearly in my spirit. Sometimes I ache to hear You, but all I hear is the wind blowing outside, the refrigerator making noises, and the silence of this room."

My mind wandered to and fro; I wanted to write something that would make my Lord smile, but my mind drew a blank. In my restlessness, I sensed I was hungry, so I ate a few crackers. There I was, waiting, writing about nothing significant and waiting for something, though I was not sure what. Have you ever felt like you were waiting for something but not sure what it was?

I whispered a prayer: "Lord, speak to me. Open my spiritual ears. Change me from the inside out."

Beloved, joy is yours, My gift to you: the delight of resting in My presence as I enjoy just being with you. You wonder why I would enjoy such a seemingly meaningless event from your perspective. Look again. I created you for the sole purpose of fellowship with Me, and when you slow down and stop the frantic activities of life and desire that fellowship with Me as well, I am filled with joy. Believe Me when I tell you that intimacy of soul is a two-way blessing, yours and Mine. Yes, this is true; do not doubt.

I call you My friend, and you are. I also call you My child, which you are. And I call you My beloved, which is also true. Rejoice in this mystery revealed to you. I desire all My children to grasp this reality and truth for each one personally.

Abraham believed Me, and I counted that as sufficient, right in fellowship with Me even when he messed up and didn't trust Me in seasons of weakness and fear because of his humanness, the fallen state of all mankind. Like you, though, he realized this, repented and drew near to Me again by believing I live,

The Blessing Of Believing God

I see, I know all and that My promises are true and faithful. This honors Me. For the sake of the honor of My name I will also fulfill My promise of life and blessing and purpose I have for My children. Believe. Look up and receive your continual redemption: sanctification in Jesus Christ. Rejoice in My love.

A new song I sing over you, a song for My children. Listen:

> Joy! Joy! Joy!
> Love for My Beloved
> Brings Me joy, joy, joy!
> Can you see My love for you?
> Look for Me in all you do,
> I am here, always true.
> I love you, My Beloved.
> Walk in joy and truth.
>
> Power flows from My hand.
> The words in My mouth
> Bring life and light, peace, and hope,
> To those who cry to Me for help.
>
> Joy I give to you, Beloved.
> Stay with Me a while.
> Walk with Me and stay so near.

God Still Speaks

Watch and see what I will do.

Believe, Beloved.
Dream, Beloved.
Always seek My face.
My Word is life.
My presence is power.
My name is on you, Beloved.

Walk in joy.
Walk in truth.
Walk in love and power.
I am yours, you are Mine, Beloved!

Reflections

Chapter 26
CARRYING ANOTHER'S BURDEN

> Carry each other's burdens, and in this way you will fulfill the law of Christ. (Galatians 6:2)

I was driving into work. My heart was heavy for a dear friend of mine struggling greatly with financial hardship and intense physical pain. I was talking to God about this and praying fervently for a miracle. Then, in my soul, I clearly heard the Lord say, "I love her more than you do. Trust Me." I was hushed by this profound truth. My eyes welled with tears.

Soon a song rose up within me, as if God was singing to me to encourage my soul and strengthen me to continue to trust Him. It was a song of God's faithful love for us. I was able to talk to my friend the following day and encourage her with what God said to me. How valuable friendship is! What a gift to know that we never walk alone.

Carrying Another's Burden

I think back to the immensely difficult seasons I have gone through in my life and how during those times others have faithfully prayed for me and encouraged me with notes, texts, phone calls, and visits. What a divine gift to be able to come alongside a friend and help carry their burden. It always ends up being a double blessing, both for the encourager and for the one being encouraged. Both are strengthened in the spirit and by what God ultimately does in the situation.

Over time we can look back and see how God's grace and the friendships of those dear to us carried us through. Being reminded that God loves each of us far more than we could ever love those most dear to us made me consider again how Christ Himself paid for all our sins on the cross, a debt we could never have paid on our own. His resurrection from the dead then displayed His awesome power to save us even from death. He bears our daily burdens and carries us through the darkest storms of life. I opened my journal and read something the Lord had given to me a few weeks earlier:

> Beloved, knowing the truth of My love for My own and knowing My power is over all authorities in all creation is key to living a life of peace. Regardless of whether life is hard or easy, regardless of whether things are going your way or not, I love My own.

At times My children get very discouraged when I don't answer their prayer as they have outlined for Me to perform. They may even think I have rejected them when things go terribly wrong. They sometimes cry out in anger or despair, "I was faithful to God, and He let this happen to me!" To this response I say, "I am the Lord God of all creation. Fear not. Nothing I allow in all the earth is for the destruction of My bride, the church, but only to bring forth her holiness that My glory would be revealed to all the earth."

Concerning those whom you love, dear one, fear not. I am the faithful One, He who loves perfectly. All that I allow is to draw a soul to My merciful heart and to reveal My awesome power and eternal love. Do not be shortsighted, but see with kingdom eyes.

See My kingdom advancing on the earth. See the day of the Lord drawing near. Fear not. I will make a way where there appears to be no solution to the problem. I redeem all that the enemy has destroyed and crushed. The hope of My Beloved is a most tender thing to Me; I will redeem it. The faith of one of My children is like precious gold and gems to Me; I will guard it and protect it. I will bring about the restoration of their faith in My love, goodness, and authority. Do not doubt.

It is not meant that you understand everything I allow, for My authority is over all that exists. The enemy does have dominion over places on the Earth, for it is a fallen world as a result of mankind's sin. But be of good cheer: I have overcome the evil one. I have overcome death. I have overcome the world.

I have overcome all sin for the redemption of all creation. I am reclaiming all that was lost to the enemy since the fall of man in the Garden of Eden. I am recreating, restoring, rebuilding for My Father's glory. You, too, will praise My Father for His awesome and perfect plan.

Meanwhile, while Satan still has authority over places in the earth, do not think that he is not under My authority. Recall the book of Job in My holy Scriptures. All will bring forth My glory. Wait and see what I will do. Eyes of faith are required. Prayers of faith are critical. The prayers of My saints strengthen My kingdom forces in the heavenly realms and on the earth. Your eyes will see it, and you will be amazed.

Life is more than food and drink. Life is meant to be wrapped up in all Christ died for you to have. Choose this path daily. Even when you see evil in the world, choose to believe My kingdom is advancing, and My saints are praising Me for My power, authority, and faithful provision. Manna from heaven and water from the rock is not too hard for Me. But I will share My glory with no one. Lay down your pride daily, for indeed nothing is possible apart from what I grant. Every skill and ability, every word of wisdom, every song of joy, and all music of beauty—these are from My hand, intended to bring Me glory and to bless My people. Financial provision is also from My hand.

I know what each of My own needs daily, and I will provide it, including the refining fire that brings forth holiness in My people. All who seek Me with a pure heart shall

Carrying Another's Burden

see Me and rejoice. So many of My children are spoiled or disillusioned by the ways of the world and by their thinking that is contrary to My Word. Therefore, I must cleanse the house of God, My church, of all unrighteousness and teach My people anew who I am: My character, My power, My provision, My authority, My love, and My mercy. I am holy.

Do not despise what I allow to teach My people these amazing truths. Each one is on their own unique faith path with Me. Some will curse Me, some will cry out to Me, some will run to Me quickly, and some will stay in My arms of grace. Pray for all of them, dear one, for indeed it is true: life bursts forth when My people pray in the authority and power of My perfect son, Jesus Christ.

Reflections

Chapter 27
HOLY WEEK

> Then he (Jesus) placed his right hand on me and said: "Do not be afraid. I am the First and the Last. I am the Living One; I was dead, and now look, I am alive for ever and ever!" (Revelation 1:17-18)

When I was young I looked forward to Easter as a day of family gatherings, special meals, coloring Easter eggs, and lots of chocolate to eat. For many years I did not grasp the true wonder of this celebration. But I have learned and now am compelled to share why Easter is to me now the most blessed day of celebration and what this day is meant to cause us to seriously reflect on.

Consider Good Friday. It was the day of the bitter passion of Jesus the Christ, the Son of God who was rejected by men. God knew we could not redeem ourselves for our sins against Him, so He sent us Jesus. All of the sins of all mankind were laid upon Jesus while He hung on the cross. The Bible calls Jesus the

Holy One, the Lamb of God who takes away the sins of the world (John 1:29). Jesus became the Passover Lamb, a key reference in The Old Testament, the innocent one sacrificed for the redemption and forgiveness of all mankind for their rebellion against God. God's punishment upon us all for our sins and rejection of His ways would 'pass over' us. The full wrath of God's judgment was put on Jesus as He hung on the cross–a most bitter cup of anguish. That is when Jesus cried out, "Abba Father, why have you forsaken me?"

It was then that, for the first and only time, Jesus was not only completely alone but completely separated from Almighty God. God the Father looked away from His Son so that Jesus could bear the fullness of that burden alone. Jesus did this willingly because He understood what it would accomplish: our redemption. This is what Jesus Christ accomplished on the cross for all of mankind. This is why Christians call it Good Friday, because Jesus Christ brought perfect reconciliation between God and mankind. Then Jesus died, finishing that which He was born to accomplish. The veil in the temple was torn in two from top to bottom, representing that man was no longer separated from God. Then they laid Him in the tomb, and a stone was rolled in front of it. All was still.

HOLY WEEK

We call the following Sunday Easter. We who love Jesus call it Resurrection Day. When Jesus emerged alive in the body from the tomb, all of heaven was praising God for the astounding mercy and grace poured out on mankind. There must have been great rejoicing, and a triumphant shout! And I believe God smiled. Jesus appeared many times in the flesh over the next forty days to His disciples, including once to over five hundred people at one time (1 Corinthians 15:6).

What incomprehensible joy! Because of what Jesus accomplished, nothing could ever again separate humankind from relationship with God Almighty. Jesus conquered death and the grave. For all who would believe Jesus is the Christ, the Messiah, the Son of God, there is perfect forgiveness of all sin and rebellion. This is why Easter is the most blessed day of celebration to Christians. Jesus restored what was destroyed in the Garden of Eden when mankind first rebelled against God. I always find great joy in the words He spoke: "Behold, I make all things new" (Revelation 21:5).

Powerful light and life burst forth from Jesus that resurrection morning. That light and life still bursts forth today. The Spirit of the living God raised Jesus from the death of the body. Triumph! Victory! For all who would simply believe, the gift of God's perfect love, eternal life, is free. This I believe, and this has transformed my life in the most powerful, joyous, and surprising ways. He walks with me and talks with me. Who would believe my report if I would tell all the details of my relationship with God of the universe? It keeps me in reverent awe and wonder.

Some may ask, "What is the motivation that would cause the God of all the universe to do such an astonishing thing?" God tells us the answer in John 3:16–17: "For God so loved the world that He gave His one and only Son, that whoever believes in Him shall not perish but have eternal life. For God did not send His Son into the world to condemn the world, but to save the world through Him."

In my quiet time with God over the last sixteen years, He has moved upon my heart to write in my journal about many things. Concerning His motivation to send His Son Jesus into the world to save His creation, this is what He spoke to my heart, which I feel I am to share with you:

> Write of My love for all people. Tell them of My extravagant love. They do not know the depths of My love for My creation. Who but I have given My Beloved Son for the redemption of all mankind, the blood of My Son to cover the sins of the whole world?

Holy Week

Who but I have raised My Son from the dead to prove to all peoples that He is My Son and all He said is true?

What other god has relentlessly pursued his own to call them back from their rebellion and make a way of reconciliation between us? Has any other god demonstrated such love, justice, mercy, and righteousness? No.

My power cannot be matched by anyone else, for I created all things seen and unseen. Nothing compares to My eternal love for My own. I continue to reveal Myself to My people, but they are so distracted and misled by the ways of the world. When will they turn their hearts back to Me? Tell them I live, tell them I love them, and tell them what you have learned and experienced personally with Me, the Living God of all.

And so I respond with reverent awe, "Yes, Lord, I will tell all who will listen. If only one will believe, then I will still speak."

Reflections

Chapter 28
GOD'S PEACE IN THE SEASON OF GRIEVING

> Peace I leave with you; my peace I give you. I do not give to you as the world gives. Do not let your hearts be troubled and do not be afraid. (John 14:27)

Like you, some days I struggle to stay focused on the important things, especially when I feel tired or overwhelmed. It is on these days I often need some quiet space, some alone time to rest my mind. But out of habit I often keep doing things—some necessary tasks like making meals and cleaning the kitchen, but more often than not things of little importance. Sometimes this is fine. I want to catch up on emails and browse social media to hear from family and friends. The workroom always seems to need straightening up. But on this particular day I felt unsettled inside. I was sad.

My oldest brother, Bob, died unexpectedly in 2015, and I am still navigating through my journey of grief.

He and I had a very unique relationship. You see, Bob was disabled, developmentally delayed, and I cared for him off and on the last thirty-three years of his life. Our relationship was more like a parent–child relationship than it was a sibling one. I loved him very much.

I miss Bob and the quirky conversations we often had. He required very little and always just wanted to be accepted and loved by others. He was a gentle soul, a quiet man, generally, unless he was talking about his one passion: trains. I am so grateful that just two weeks before he died, I spent two days with him as he was in the hospital recovering from surgery. Interestingly, he asked me many questions that day about God and heaven. He had only done this once or twice previously. He said he was looking forward to seeing Mom and Dad, our sister Kathy, and other loved ones who had passed away. He always wanted to have a big family reunion and thought heaven would be like that. He told me he believed Jesus was God's son and that Jesus died for us and God raised Him from the dead. "That is why we get to go to heaven," he said. I was so joyful this conversation occurred. I had no idea it would be the last time I would see Bob alive.

For weeks after Bob's untimely and sudden death, there was so much to do: determining where to bury him, planning his memorial, calling and writing his friends to tell them he was gone. Then there was the necessary work of going through all his personal belongings. It was a time-consuming task and emotionally wearying, boxing up pictures, packing up many things to be donated, discarding countless things that were important and meaningful only to him. He must have kept every card and letter anyone had ever sent him. There were tender moments when I would discover things about him as I read notes on little pieces of paper he had written to himself and saved. I consolidated his entire lifetime into two little boxes that I will keep. It was very sobering.

My natural tendency is to stay busy, but once the critical tasks were completed, I suffered serious back spasms that forced me to rest for over a week. I think my body knew I needed time to be alone and grieve. Memories resurfaced of when other loved ones had died—an unborn child, my sister, Mom, Dad, and some dear friends. Shortly after Bob died, our precious dog, Tasha, got cancer, and two months later she too was gone. She had been deeply integrated into our lives for thirteen years. Now, the house was quiet. It was so very hard to say goodbye.

I had written little about these things in my journal. Sometimes it takes me a long time to process what happens in my life. Perhaps it just hurt too much, and I got tired of being weepy. I needed to hear from God, hear His perspective. But so often I could not hear; at times, heaven seemed silent. It was hard to read the Bible and pray.

During that time most friends didn't ask me about Bob or Tasha very often, I presume because they didn't want to make me sad. But I was sad inside anyway, and talking about it just disabled my ability to hide the tears. You have your own stories like this. Different names, but the pain is just as deep. I find my healing by seeking God, and gratefully, I have found that God seeks me out when I can't make my way to His arms of grace.

An entry in my journal written a few months after Bob died means so very much to me. The pattern is now common in my life and evidence of the way God always meets me in my pain with His tender love and precious peace when I wait in His presence.

> Write words of life, words of hope. Write words of truth to encourage souls, for life is hard, and the evil one desires to crush hope, distort truth, mislead, and confuse souls.
>
> I, the Lord, desire that souls would live in perfect relationship with Me, shielded from the horror of being eternally separated from the living God of all creation.

I desire that you live triumphantly, Beloved. Not tired, exhausted, or weary as you are. Yes, grief is a natural response to the death of a loved one. Bob beat you to heaven. Rejoice in his eternal happiness! He is perfect now; there are no disabilities in heaven. Although it is very hard, try to focus more on your heavenly home than on the empty space in your life now that he is with Me in paradise. I will help you.

My plan is perfect, Beloved. My timing is perfect. I am never late, never early. Do not try to rationalize why I took Bob home so soon from your perspective. Trust Me with all of your unanswered questions. I will help you. I wipe the tears from your eyes. Not one tear escapes My notice. I am near to the brokenhearted.

Now rest. Rest your heart and your soul. You need to just soak in the calm of My presence. I am your Prince of Peace. I am He who loves you perfectly and eternally. Rest in this truth.

Jesus said…"I am the resurrection and the life. The one who believes in me will live, even though they die." (John 11:25)

Reflections

Chapter 29
WHAT DOES IT MEAN TO REALLY BELIEVE GOD?

> Jesus said to him, "If you can believe, all things are possible to him who believes."
> (Mark 9:23 NKJV)

Over the course of my journey in striving to know God and learning how to walk closer with Him, I have often struggled with my small faith and inconsistent ability to trust and believe Him. I would say in my heart and with my words that I believed God, and then I would find myself at the end of a day looking back and being disappointed with myself in how little I had talked to God or that I had behaved in a manner that clearly showed I did not trust Him completely.

The Lord continuously encourages me to not allow guilt to get in the way of quickly reengaging with Him, returning to intimacy of soul with Him. He shows me in the Scriptures His great love for us, His unrelenting pursuit of relationship with us, and His mercy, patience, and tremendous power to save. I do great for a couple of hours or days, and then, so often, I stumble in my faith.

So it is not surprising that a recurring theme has been woven throughout our conversations over these many years: believing Him. When I pick up a journal from fifteen years ago, He is speaking to me about rejecting the lies of the world and choosing instead to believe Him. My journal entries from recent years still include phrases like "Believe Me" and "Resist doubt and partial belief."

A few years ago, as I was driving alone in my car for a weekend away with a few girlfriends, I was listening to music and talking with Jesus. I then heard Him in the spirit say, *"What would it be like if you believed Me about everything?"* It was more than a passing thought. My mind and entire being awoke as He spoke:

> "What would it be like, Beloved?
> What would your life be like if you believed Me about everything I have ever said?
> What would *you* be like?
> How would it change our relationship?

> Consider all the words I have ever spoken to you, little one—all the words I have revealed in the holy Scriptures. What would it be like if you believed Me—*really believed Me*—about everything?"

These questions echoed in my spirit throughout much of that day and in the following weeks, months, and years. I contemplated the depth of what He was asking me, prayed for greater faith, and spoke with close friends about the challenge to really, really believe God. I hungered to believe God about everything and regularly asked Him to help me to be faithful to Him and to increase the capacity of my faith.

Three years later, to my surprise and delight, He answered that question for me on a quiet evening when I was all alone.

> Now, what *would* it look like if you *really* believed Me about *everything* I have ever said?
> You would experience the miraculous and supernatural every day.
> You would see what I am doing all around you, and be continually amazed!
> Your prayers would be answered in ways you would not expect but would always bring Me glory.

What Does It Mean To Really Believe God?

> You would pray for *impossible* things for the purpose of advancing the kingdom of God here on earth.
>
> You would walk as Jesus walked: in perfect alignment with God the Father at all times.
>
> You would not doubt My love and authority.
>
> You would recognize the lies of the enemy and reject them instantly.
>
> You would still experience the hardships of life, for you still live in a fallen world, but your eyes would be focused on your heavenly home and your eternal reward.
>
> You would live fully each day and sleep peacefully at night.
>
> You would have clarity of mind, vivid thoughts, and understanding about people I bring you to for ministering My life to them that they would know I live, I see, I know every motive and thought of all.

That was two years ago. Of no surprise, last month He again challenged me saying,

> "Unwavering trust is needed, heavenly perspective is required. Just what would it be like if you really believed Me about

everything? It would change everything! Allow Me the freedom to change everything for My Father's glory."

My eyes fill with tears of optimism as I again whisper my recurring prayer, "Please Lord, heal me of all unbelief concerning Your Word."

Reflections

Chapter 30
WHEN GOD SINGS

> The Lord your God is with you, he is mighty to save. He will take great delight in you, he will quiet you with his love, he will rejoice over you with singing. (Zephaniah 3:17)

I don't know about you, but I go through seasons where I am so intently aware of God's presence–conversing with Him throughout my busy days, enjoying His company in quiet times during my commute to and from work, reading the Bible in the still of the morning with anticipation, and journaling when my heart is stirred to write.

And then I get consumed with work, projects, challenges, or life activities. I realize I have not been paying very much attention to my relationship with God. It usually happens slowly, subtly, a little bit at a time. It is kind of like how one enjoys regular chats with dear friends and then you realize you have not talked for weeks on end. You tell yourself you need to call them and catch up or go visit. Then somehow, the months slip by and you wonder, "Where did the time go? I miss them!"

Is it that we become complacent, assuming there is always tomorrow and they will always be there and will understand we have been busy? Most of the time, they do understand. But sadly, some relationships wither due to lack of attention.

When I realize I have neglected my time with Jesus, I often pull out one of my journals and start reading, and I am always stunned by how close I was with the Lord *then* and how much I miss that closeness with Him *now*. I open my Bible and start reading, hungry to reengage with God.

This reengagement occurred again recently. Does this happen to you, too? I am embarrassed to admit how often this cycle occurs in my life. I began thanking God for His mercies, His faithfulness, and the perfection of what Jesus Christ did for me on the cross to pay the price of my rebellion against Father God. I found myself worshiping Him for overcoming death by His resurrection, praising Him for the eternal life He gives us.

I began to weep because I was acutely aware that I had become too casual in my relationship with Him, taking for granted the wondrous gift He has given me:

the gift to be able to commune with Him, the Creator of the universe. I became aware of how much it wounds Him when His people wander away from relationship with Him, ignore Him, dismiss Him, and neglect His Word. I began to thank Him for His patience with us, His people, His patience with me.

You may know that all those who believe and receive the profound gift of reconciliation Jesus provided are often referred to in the New Testament as "the bride of Christ." I reflected upon this reference of such a tender relationship. I wept that we take His love for us for granted, that so many really don't grasp the extensiveness of His love for us. I was then overcome with His peace and I heard in my heart:

> Beloved, a new song I give to you today, as your heart has grown tender toward Me once again. Your complacency toward the gift that I have so generously poured into you has been cast down and exposed.

Sing the new song that I have for My bride the church, the church whom I love:

> Come back to Me, My people.
> Come back to Me, My child.
> Turn your face to Me, My son.

When God Sings

You are My people, My children.
You are My people, My bride.
I want you to know and understand
I am your God. I love you more,
more than you know.

Come back to Me, My people.
Turn your face to Me.
Open your eyes to the beauty of My face,
the wonders of My grace,
the power of My Word.

Return to Me, My people.
Run to My arms of grace!
Bow before My holiness. Seek My face.

Return to Me, My people,
soften your hearts toward Me.
Lay down your pride and unbelief,
look up, and see Me.
My love for you is still real.
My love for you is powerful.
My love for you is great and mighty to save.

I love you! I love you,
with every beat of My heart.
Return to Me, My people.
Return to Me, My child.

Joy fills My heart as you turn to Me!
Joy fills My heart as you bow in humility.
Joy fills My heart as I speak life to you:
Return to Me, Beloved, I love you.

Joy fills My heart
as you weep tears before Me,
as you realize the ways you have rebelled.
Joy fills My heart
as you repent and run to Me!
Joy fills My heart, My child.

I abundantly pour into you: life, joy, truth!
Joy fills My heart
as you return to Me, My child.

Be strong in Christ My Son.
Be strong in the Spirit of My power.
Be strong in My truth, My Word.
Be strong in Me.

Joy fills My heart as you return to Me!
Joy fills My heart as you lift your eyes.
As you lay down your pride,
as you submit to Me,
Joy fills My heart, and I speak to you life!
I speak to you life: Life in Christ! Life in Me!
Joy!

When God Sings

Hear the song I sing to you, Beloved.
Joy fills My heart to sing this song.
I love you My Bride, I love you!
Come boldly to My throne.

(Amos 5:4, Isaiah 44:22, Jeremiah 24:7,
Joel 2:12, Zechariah 1:3)

Reflections

Chapter 31
A CALL TO AWAKEN

> Furthermore, knowing the time, now is the moment to awake from sleep. For now our salvation is nearer than when we first believed. (Romans 13:11 MEV)

Increasingly over the last few years when I am quiet in His presence, I hear in my spirit God calling His people to wake up. At first I didn't understand the reference, but it has become clear to me that from His perspective, most people are in a spiritual coma, a deep sleep, and are oblivious to the things of God.

Perhaps we are too busy, overwhelmed, or disillusioned by the harshness of life. We are sometimes distraught due to tragic events, and can grow blind to, or numb to our need for God. Some have given up on God; they have been wounded too deeply and find themselves choosing to believe He does not care about this world or about them personally, and some have chosen to believe He just does not exist.

But He does exist. He has proved it to me throughout my life. He has changed my life in wondrous ways.

Like you, I allow my schedule to get too busy and full. I sometimes get depressed. I am deeply grieved when those I love battle diseases or die. I am hurt when I am misunderstood. I can get overwhelmed due to the insanity of what I hear on the news and see on TV. I sometimes fall back into the old, familiar habit of escaping from these things by zoning out and watching old movies for hours or throwing myself into my work. But over the last four decades of learning how to live the Christian life, I have found that the faster I turn to God for help, hope, and grace, the faster my mind, spirit, and soul find peace and strength for the day at hand.

I don't have all the answers to all my questions, but I have learned I can trust God completely with all that my mind cannot grasp. He has proven Himself to be trustworthy, faithful, merciful, and strong enough to carry me through this life into eternity. This is more than sufficient for me.

The most surprising parts of my spiritual journey in learning to know God have been the astounding realizations of how real He really is, how much He loves us, how incredibly close He is, and that He still speaks. How awesome in power He is, the expanse of His wisdom, how He is continually revealing Himself to us, and how He relentlessly pursues us with His extravagant love. It is meant to be a lifelong journey, a process, a daily response to the pursuit of Him who loves us, and a striving to know the truth from God's perspective.

As I considered how to close this book, God compelled me to write in my journal, and the resulting love letter flowed onto the page. My prayer is that you, too, would awaken to God's Spirit and ask Him to help you on your own spiritual journey to know and love Him with all of your heart, all of your mind, and all of your soul. Yes, it is possible! But it requires intent and focus. It is a daily choice and a wondrous lifelong journey. I pray that you also would choose this astounding path of life.

> Words of life I have for My people.
> Are you listening for My voice?
>
> Unstop your ears and lean toward Me;
> strain to hear the truths I have for you.
>
> Why do you not walk in power?
> It is because My Word is not alive in you.
>
> Why is this so? Because you do not know and love My Word more than you love the ways and words of the world.

My Spirit is the Spirit of love, power, and a disciplined mind.

The enemy of the kingdom of God, the enemy of your soul, is the spirit of fear, timidity, confusion, destruction, and death. The battle is constant, for the enemy does not sleep. I also do not sleep. Whom are you listening to?

Why do you doubt Me and the power of My Word?

Why do you not expect miracles every day because of Christ in you? Because you are immune to My presence. You are more interested in pleasing people, being noticed, and fulfilling the goals and plans you have made. You know all the trivia of TV shows and current events but you do not know Me, the living God of all creation.

I still speak.
I still hear.

I still see all that transpires in the world, in your life, and in your heart. Nothing escapes My notice.

You resist Me without knowing it because you are not desperate for Me. When will you be hungry for intimacy of soul with your Creator?

Scour My Word, the Bible, and you will see that from the beginning of time I have revealed Myself to My creation and spoken to My people. Continually I speak, and continually I desire communion with you, dialogue in the spirit, unity of mind and purpose.

Ask Me each moment what I desire to do and say to you and to those you interact with.

Never forget that I am holy. And you also, My people: you are to be holy. Search the Scriptures to understand what this means, for you do not know what it means to walk in holiness, to have holy thoughts and holy speech. It should not be so.

My Spirit says to you, "Awaken!" Cast off the clothes of apathy, despair, and pride. You resist Me even now as you hear My words; you think you are fine and that I am speaking to others and not to you. Repent, Beloved. Humble yourself before My authority. Prostrate yourself before Me, and ask Me to expose to you what I see in your life and in your heart.

> Believe Me when I say
> My return draws near.
> Prepare yourself.
> Run to Me!
> I love you.
> I Am The Lord.

(Mark 12:24, 2 Timothy 1:7, Acts 1:11, Ephesians 5:14)

Reflections

Conclusion
THE TIME TO BELIEVE IS NOW

> I tell you, now is the time of God's favor, now is the day of salvation.
> (2 Corinthians 6:2b)

Over these many years I have learned that faith is to be walked out each day by choosing to cultivate a personal and relevant relationship with Almighty God. The awesome news is this is possible! However, I have learned that it must be done intentionally–it does not just 'happen'. Like any relationship, it can be neglected.

I have learned we cannot be 'good enough' to get into heaven, no matter how hard we try. This is contrary to how I was raised which made parts of my spiritual journey quite bumpy. It is very hard for some people to accept this as most religions have many requirements, rules, even levels of achievement to attain right standing with God. But thankfully in the Bible,

The Time To Believe Is Now

Ephesians 2:8–9 proclaims, "For it is by grace you have been saved, through faith—and this is not from yourselves, it is the gift of God—not by works, so that no one can boast."

Imagine that! We just have to believe what the Bible says. We just have to accept what the Bible says about Jesus.

Jesus proclaimed, "I am the way and the truth and the life. No one comes to the Father except through me" (John 14:6).

Yes, Jesus became flesh and boldly declared the truth of the Scriptures—God's ways, motives, and intentions to reconcile all of mankind to Himself. What a gift! But this requires each person to receive God's gift. Don't leave the unopened package on the shelf, never knowing the wondrous treasure inside!

Jesus says in John 16:27, "The Father himself loves you because you have loved me and have believed that I came from God."

Like all believers, I stumble regularly, but I still strive to walk humbly with God each day, relying on His love and mercy demonstrated in Jesus Christ. Every day I must choose to believe God's Word and talk with Him. How astonishing that God knew we would stumble and fall, backslide and neglect Him…and yet He made a plan to save us anyway. A letter the Lord inspired me to write is an encouragement to us all:

> I am the Lord God Almighty. I am the God of life; hear My words. The enemy of the Lord destroys, but I save those who call out to Me and diligently seek Me with all their heart.
>
> I am the light of the world. I am the bread of life. Why do My people not seek me? Because many are deceived by the pleasures of this world, and wickedness has crept into their hearts, making them cold toward Me and loving the ways of the world more than My ways.
>
> Abundant life is yours as you trust Me and believe My Word of truth. When you trust and believe Me, you obey My words of life. You quickly forgive those who wound you and run to Me for all you need. You rely on Me to love others unconditionally through you. You lay aside your pride, your plans, your preconceived ideas of what your day, your career, your life should look like, even how much money you feel you need to

make. I know better than you, little one, exactly what you need to thrive.

No longer be satisfied with just surviving, just living. I died for you and rose from the dead so that you would have abundant life. This means experiencing My power, My joy, and My peace every day, even when things are not going as you'd like.

I am never late. My plan and purposes are eternally very good for My kingdom. You are part of that as you trust Me and obey, humbling yourself before Me; it is then that you can thrive in My presence.

Now is the time to believe Me and not to doubt when I am slow to act, in your opinion. Today is the day to look up and claim your reward: the joy of the Lord is your strength! Keep your eyes set on eternity for this life on Earth is fleeting; like a wisp of smoke it passes. Only My Word remains forever. Amen.

I whisper a prayer, "Lord God I choose to believe you today. Cleanse me from all unrighteousness. Continually draw me near to your merciful heart, and lead me in the way of everlasting life."

And so my journey of faith continues;
what a wondrous and mysterious journey it is…

Reflections

REFERENCES

Endorsements:
Bishop Cleophas B. Makona, C/O RTJCM-AFRICA P.O.BOX 3629-30200 Kitale, Kenya Africa Affiliated with Christ For First Nations http://www.christforfirstnations.com/index.php?id=21

Introduction:
Warner, Anna Bartlett. Jesus Loves Me This I Know. 1859.

Chapter 1:
Warren, Rick. 2002. The Purpose Driven Life: What on earth am I here for? Zondervan. www.purpose-driven.com

Feinberg, Margaret. 2011. Hungry For God: Hearing God's Voice in the Ordinary and the Everyday. Zondervan. www.margaretfeinberg.com

Chapter 4:
Saint Maria Faustina Kowalska. 2002. Diary: Divine Mercy in my Soul. Marians of the Immaculate Conception.

Chapter 9:

The One Year Bible: The entire New Living Translation arranged into 365 daily readings. 2004. Tyndale House Publishers, Inc.

Chapter 19:

Bible Study Fellowship (BSF). www.bsfinternational.org

California Women's Retreat. www.cawr.org

Other Bible Versions Used

In addition to New International Version (NIV), scripture was sourced from:

New King James Version (NKJV).
  Copyright 1982 by Thomas Nelson.

English Standard Version (ESV).
  Copyright 2001 by Crossway.

Good News Translation (GNT).
  Copyright 1992 American Bible Society.

Modern English Version (MEV).
  Copyright 2014 by Military Bible Association.

New Living Translation (NLT).
  Copyright 1996, 2004, 2015 by Tyndale House Foundation.

CPSIA information can be obtained
at www.ICGtesting.com
Printed in the USA
FSHW012051160519
58200FS